WITHDRAWN

LEONCE AND LENA
LENZ · WOYZECK

GERMAN LITERARY CLASSICS
IN TRANSLATION
General Editor: KENNETH J. NORTHCOTT

Georg Büchner
LEONCE AND LENA; LENZ; WOYZECK
Translated by Michael Hamburger

SELECTED POEMS OF
FRIEDRICH HÖLDERLIN AND EDUARD MÖRIKE
Translated by Christopher Middleton

J. M. R. Lenz
THE TUTOR and THE SOLDIERS
Translated by William E. Yuill

Gotthold Ephraim Lessing
MINNA VON BARNHELM
Translated by Kenneth J. Northcott

Friedrich von Schiller
WILHELM TELL
Translated by W. F. Mainland

Georg Büchner

LEONCE AND LENA
LENZ · WOYZECK

Translated
with an
Introduction
and Notes by
MICHAEL
HAMBURGER

The University of Chicago Press
Chicago and London

The University of Chicago Press, Chicago 60637
The University of Chicago Press, Ltd., London

International Standard Book Number:
0–226–07841–8, (clothbound)
Library of Congress Catalog Card Number: 78–184507

CONTENTS

INTRODUCTION

German literature is rich in isolated, anachronistic, scarcely accountable achievements, but none is more extraordinary than that of Georg Büchner, who died in 1837 at the age of twenty-three. Büchner was isolated, because he had no use for the artistic, cultural, and philosophical assumptions of his German contemporaries or for the aristocratic-bourgeois social order on which they rested. Büchner was anachronistic, because his literary practice owed little or nothing to the Romanticism, Neoclassicism, or tendentious topicality of his immediate predecessors and coevals, but linked up with the *Sturm und Drang* of the 1770s—and through it with the example of Shakespeare—yet went so far beyond any precedent that his work did not begin to be appreciated until half a century after his death. Büchner's achievement is scarcely accountable, because, a scientist by training and profession, he succeeded in writing plays effective on the stage in the midst of activities and preoccupations that left him no time for a theatrical or literary apprenticeship. It was Büchner's innate talent or genius that made him the only German dramatist of his period whose plays have not only survived both as theater and as literature but have grown more important, more relevant with the passage of time and of countless movements, trends, and fashions.

The fact that Büchner was a political revolutionary, more radical in his thinking about society than the liberal reformers of the Young Germany group to which his friend and supporter Karl Gutzkow belonged, has a great deal to do with Büchner's originality as an imaginative writer. It has to do with his choice of heroes or antiheroes—from Danton in his first play to Lenz and Woyzeck—and with the realism that made him draw so much of his material from documentary evidence. These two distinctions of Büchner's art would have been enough to turn him into a precursor of the Naturalist school, as he was amongst other things, and to set him apart from the Romanticism and Neoclassicism of his time; but they would not have been enough to save his works from the danger to which most of his politically and socially conscious contemporaries, including Gutzkow, succumbed, the danger of tendentious topicality.

Büchner's realism was something other, rarer and deeper than social or political awareness. It was a quality of insight, imagination, and compassion that he shares with the greatest writers of many different periods, almost regardless of whether those writers would have understood what is meant by realism as a literary practice. We do not read or watch *Dantons Tod* (*Danton's Death*) in order to find out what happened at a particular stage of the French Revolution, since we can do that by reading historical works like those which Büchner used as sources for much, but by no means all, of his dramatic dialogue. We do not read or watch *Woyzeck* in order to find out what happened when a barber of that name was tried and sentenced to death for murder in the 1820s, or even to get an idea of what social conditions were like in Germany in that or the following decade, although Büchner drew on his Hessian environment for much, but by no means all, of the setting and diction of his dramatic fragment. We are moved by those plays because they give us "the thing itself," not in the Kantian sense, which Büchner rejected as he rejected every kind of philosophical idealism, but in the Shakespearean sense when King Lear speaks of "unaccommodated man" as a "poor, bare, forked animal." Büchner's realism is inseparable from his tragic sense of life, and his tragic sense of life sprang from his total involvement in the condition of unaccommodated man as a poor, bare, forked animal. King Lear himself was reduced to that recognition by political circumstances and events. The same is true of Büchner, as his letters testify, but his political commitment and experience do not account for the intensity and penetration of his poetic vision. What is just as significant as Büchner's borrowings from documentary sources is the close parallel between certain crucial speeches in his imaginative works and passages in his personal letters. In other words, Büchner's realism was as much a product of his peculiar sensibility as it was a literary method.

This can be seen most clearly in Büchner's comedy *Leonce und Lena*, because its outer framework derives from a Romantic convention, that of the fairy-tale play, as written in Germany by Ludwig Tieck, and the *comédie-proverbe* of Alfred de Musset. Yet Büchner's tragic sense of life, his constant preoccupation with unaccommodated man, permitted no more than formal concessions to the comic medium. For all its lightness of touch, *Leonce und Lena* is more explicit than Büchner's other imaginative works about the stripping down of human beings to "the thing itself." Büchner needed no thunderstorm and no blasted heath, no revolution, murder, or madness to render his vision of extremity, since it was in extremity, in exposure, that he felt the truth about human life to lie. If *Leonce und Lena* is no less revolutionary and subversive a play than *Dantons Tod* or *Woyzeck*, what makes it so is not so much the satire that turns German idealistic philosophy and German monarchy into a single target—in the person of King Peter— as the questions it asks about social and moral conventions generally. Leonce and Valerio, the prince and the vagabond, are alike in having seen through them all, and where they meet is the brink of the same abyss. The comic framework forbids them to leap into it, as Woyzeck, Lenz, Danton, and his friends leap into it, but the alternative is almost more devastating: the freedom that Leonce had gone out to seek is cruelly mocked by the farcical ending, the voluntary return of Leonce and Lena to the very condition that had been imposed on them in the first place.

Büchner's obsession with this dilemma of freedom and determinism is too obvious, and has received too much critical attention, to be taken up again here. What may be worth mentioning in passing is the relevance of the obsession to Büchner's success as a dramatist, and especially as a writer of tragedies, at a time when other writers resorted to elaborate philosophical, scientific, or pseudoscientific substitutes for tragic fate. To Büchner it was not a matter of theory but of acutely experienced anguish. Since it was also a dilemma, almost certainly left unresolved at the time of his death, he could leave the crucial issues open in his plays; so much so that it is difficult to understand how the political activist of the *Hessische Landbote* (*The Hessian Courier*), the revolutionary pamphlet of which Büchner was co-author, could sustain the political impartiality of *Dantons Tod*. But this brings us back to Büchner's realism, to his uncompromising truthfulness, his psychological penetration—based on compassion—and his seemingly instinctive mastery of the art of writing.

If Büchner's realism had been nothing more than an imitation of nature—as he claimed it was in his letter of July 1835 to his parents about *Dantons Tod*, which served to rebut contemporary objections to the immorality, coarseness, and atheism of his play—the posthumous impact of his work would have been confined to the Naturalists. Dramatists and prose writers of every other school, from Hofmannsthal to Beckett, from Wedekind to Brecht, from the German Expressionists to Ionesco, could learn from Büchner's art because it was as expressive as it was mimetic. However close to the vernacular the diction of his plays and story, their effect is essentially poetic—more so, it must be added, than the effect of most of the blank verse produced by what Büchner called the "ideal poets," who offered "nothing but puppets with sky-blue noses and an affected pathos, never human beings with flesh and blood in whose pain and joy I am made to share." The *Sturm und Drang* aesthetic that Büchner derived from Shakespeare, from early Goethe, and from Lenz, whose writings on art are paraphrased in Büchner's story about him, is based on the identification of an artist with his subject, hence a projection of the subject from the inside. Language, therefore, necessarily becomes gesture; and Büchner's imaginative prose has the power to suggest more than it says, by a poetic use of rhythm and syntax that can dispense with formal eloquence, as in the case of the barely articulate Woyzeck.

The narrative prose of *Lenz* was no less unprecedented than the dialogue of *Woyzeck*, whose dramatic structure can be seen as an extreme development of the Shakespearean prototype. No writer before Büchner had attempted anything like his study of Lenz, with its documentary, casebook precision on the one hand, its projection of extreme inward states on the other. This fusion, too, and the visionary prose that renders an incipient schizophrenic's response to nature, sprang from Büchner's aesthetic of self-identification through love. Lenz himself not only formulates this aesthetic in the story—and in his own writings—but tries to carry it from art into life, to the point of wanting to revive a dead child. "One must love human nature in order to penetrate into the character of any individual; nobody, however insignificant, however ugly, should be despised; only then can one understand human nature as a whole." The historical Lenz became notorious as "Goethe's ape"; and Goethe wrote in an essay of 1776: "What the artist has not loved, does not love, he should not depict. You find the women of Rubens too fleshy? I tell you, they were *his* women, and if he'd peopled Heaven and Hell, air, earth and sea with ideals, he would have been a bad husband, and it would never have become sturdy flesh of his flesh, bone of his bone."

Yet what Büchner loved and depicted in all his works was not sturdy flesh but mental and emotional extremity, the condition of unaccommodated man. To read his letters is to come up against a pessimism difficult to reconcile with his involvement in radical politics. As early as June 1833, before his most active phase as a revolutionary, Büchner wrote to his family: "I shall always act in accordance with my principles, but have recently learnt that only the pressing need of the great majority can bring about changes, that all the commotion and shouting of individuals are folly and vanity. They write— no one reads them; they shout—no one hears them; they act —no one helps them . . ." Büchner remained committed to the victims of social and political injustice, but though his heroes and antiheroes were insignificant by the standards of an aristocratic-bourgeois order, not one of them conforms to stereotypes of the common man, the man in the street.

In *Woyzeck* it is the Captain and the Doctor who are characterized by their functions and denied the individuality of names. Their reality, for Büchner and for us, is limited by the extent to which they conform to their social functions,

falling short of full humanity because they are accommodated
—the Captain in a preconceived morality that makes him
incapable of true compassion, of true openness to the sufferings
of others, the Doctor in a pseudoscientific ideology that con-
fuses the ends and the means of knowledge. Even if we allow
for the fact that *Woyzeck* was never completed or given a
definitive shape, it remains curious that, apart from Woyzeck
and Marie, it is minor characters like the idiot Karl who were
provided with personal names. Büchner's special sympathy
with abnormal states of mind is another secret link with
Shakespeare, and particularly with *King Lear*, in which the
Fool ceases to be a mere foil to tragic majesty, and alienation,
madness, and folly become the prerequisite of authentic,
unaccommodated man. Valerio, in *Leonce und Lena*, is another
character in the lineage of Shakespeare's Fools, as the epigraph
from *As You Like It* confirms. Like the murder to which
Woyzeck is driven, madness may be the last resort of freedom
where social, political, or ideological determinism threaten to
become absolute.

Büchner's opinions and beliefs remain the subject of con-
troversy. What is clear from the evidence of his works and
letters is that, as a scientist and observer of political realities,
he recognized the primacy of material needs as a revolutionary
factor in his time. Yet even in the writing of his revolutionary
pamphlet he chose to collaborate with a clergyman. Wherever
atheism occurs in his works, from *Dantons Tod* to *Lenz*, it is
as revolt experienced with an intensity that can be described
as religious. In his scientific and philosophical writings
Büchner opposed every kind of positivism. All his imaginative
works suggest that the satisfaction of material needs alone
will not cure the existential anguish to which even his
Robespierre, the ideologist of historical determinism, and his
fairy-tale prince, Leonce, are susceptible.

If Büchner had been a didactic or tendentious writer it
would be necessary to unravel such complexities and seeming
contradictions. But the strength and universality of Büchner's
appeal does not lie on the level of opinions and beliefs. The
variety of possible responses to his works can be inferred from
the speeches of successive winners of the Büchner Prize

instituted in West Germany since the last war. Very few other German writers would have elicited so many tributes at once as idiosyncratic and as sincere as those of Günter Eich and Paul Celan, to mention no more than two of them. Only a realism as multidimensional, as intensely imaginative and psychologically penetrating, as Büchner's could have outlasted as many ephemeral realities as his work has done.

LEONCE AND LENA

A Comedy

Alfieri: "E la fama?"
Gozzi: "E la fame?"

PERSONS

KING PETER, of the kingdom of Popo

PRINCE LEONCE, his son, engaged to

PRINCESS LENA, of the kingdom of Pipi

VALERIO

GOVERNESS · TUTOR

MAJORDOMO

PRESIDENT of the Cabinet

COURT CHAPLAIN · RURAL COUNCILLOR

SCHOOLMASTER

ROSETTA

SERVANTS, MEMBERS OF THE CABINET, PEASANTS, etc.

ACT ONE

" Oh! that I were a fool !
I am ambitious for a motley coat."
AS YOU LIKE IT

SCENE ONE
A GARDEN

LEONCE, *half-reclining on a bench.* TUTOR.

LEONCE: Well, what are you after, sir? You've come to prepare
me for my vocation? I've got both my hands full with work;
I'm so busy, I don't know where to begin. You see, first of all
I've got to spit on this stone three hundred-and-sixty-five
times in succession. Have you never tried that? Then do so
now; it's quite unusually diverting. After that—do you see
this handful of sand? (*He takes up sand, throws it in the air,
and catches it on the back of his hand.*) Now I throw it into
the air. Shall we have a bet? How many grains of sand have
I got on the back of my hand? Odd or even? What! You
don't want to bet? Are you a heathen, then? Don't you
believe in God? Usually I bet with myself and can go on
with it for days. If you know where to find a person who'd
like to bet with me from time to time, I should be most
obliged to you. Then—I've got to think out a way of looking
down on my own head. If only a man could look down on
his own head! And then—and then innumerable other
occupations of the kind.—Would you say I'm an idler? Am
I not busy at this moment?—Yes, it's sad . . .
TUTOR: Very sad, Your Highness.
LEONCE: That for three weeks the clouds have been moving
from west to east. It makes me quite melancholy.
TUTOR: A very well-founded melancholy.
LEONCE: Why don't you contradict me, man? You've got
urgent business to attend to, haven't you? I'm sorry to have
detained you so long. (*The* TUTOR *retires with a low bow.*)

3

Sir, I congratulate you on the lovely parentheses formed by your legs when you bow. (*Alone,* LEONCE *stretches out on the bench.*) The bees cling so drowsily to the flowers, the sun's rays lie so lazily on the ground. A horrible idleness is spreading everywhere. Idleness is the root of every vice.—Just to think of all the things people do out of boredom! They study out of boredom, they pray out of boredom, they fall in love, marry, and procreate out of boredom and finally die of it; what's more—and that's what makes it so funny—they do it all with such a solemn expression on their faces, without knowing the reason, but attaching all sorts of weighty intentions to their pastimes. All these heroes, geniuses, and blockheads, all these saints and sinners and family men are really nothing more than sophisticated idlers.—Why, of all people, do *I* have to know it? Why don't I become important to myself, dress the poor puppet in a morning coat and put an umbrella in its hand, so as to make it very righteous, very useful and very respectable?—The man who's just left me, I envied him; I could have given him a thrashing out of pure envy. If only one could be someone else for a time. Only for a minute—(*Enter* VALERIO, *a little drunk.*) Just look how that fellow is running! I wish I knew of a single thing under the sun that could make me run at this juncture.

VALERIO: (*Walks up to the* PRINCE, *raises one finger, and stares at him fixedly.*) Yes.

LEONCE: Quite so.

VALERIO: Did you catch my meaning?

LEONCE: Perfectly.

VALERIO: All right, let's talk of something different then. (*He lies down on the grass.*) Meanwhile, I shall lie down on the grass and let my nose blossom above, amidst blades of grass; when bees and butterflies balance on it, as on a rose, may my nose derive romantic sensations from the experience.

LEONCE: Only, my excellent friend, don't sniff quite so hard, or the bees and butterflies will starve because of the monstrous pinches of snuff you're extracting from the flowers.

VALERIO: Oh, sir, how much feeling I have for nature. The grass looks so lovely that one would like to be an ox so as to be able to eat it and then again a man, so as to eat the ox that has eaten the grass.

LEONCE: Poor wretch, you too seem to be in labor with ideals.

VALERIO: The pity of it all! One can't jump off a church tower without breaking one's neck. One can't eat four pounds of cherries, stones and all, without getting stomach-ache. Look, sir, I could sit down in a corner and sing from morning till night: "Hey, there is a fly on the wall, fly on the wall, fly on the wall" and so on till the end of my days.

LEONCE: Shut up and keep your song to yourself; it's enough to drive a man mad.

VALERIO: That would be something. A madman! A madman! Who'll exchange his madness for my reason?—Ha, I'm Alexander the Great! How the sun shines a golden crown into my hair, how my uniform sparkles. Generalissimo Grasshopper, assemble the troops. Lord Spider, my Minister of Finance, I need more money. Dear Lady-in-waiting Dragonfly, how is my cherished consort, the Empress Beanstalk? Oh, my most excellent physician in ordinary, Dr. Cantharides, I am in need of a son and heir. And on top of these delicious fantasies you get good soup, good meat, good bread, a good bed to sleep on and your hair cut for nothing—in the madhouse, I mean—while I, with all my sound senses, could just about hire myself to a cherry tree for the promotion of ripeness, in order to—well?—in order to—

LEONCE: In order to make the cherries red with shame at the holes in your trousers. But, most noble sir, what about your craft, your profession, your trade, your station, your art?

VALERIO: (*With dignity.*) Sir, mine is the great business of being idle. I have acquired uncommon skill in doing nothing; I am distinguished by marvellous persistence in laziness. No callosity defiles my hands; never has the soil drunk a drop from my brow—I am still a virgin where work is concerned; and if it weren't too much trouble for me, I'd take the trouble of enlarging on my attainments for your benefit.

LEONCE: (*With comical enthusiasm.*) Let me embrace you. Are you one of those godlike ones who walk through the sweat and dust of life's highway with a pure brow, who enter

Olympus with gleaming feet and glowing bodies, like the blessed gods? Come to me, my brother in idleness!

VALERIO: (*Sings as he retires.*) "Hey, there is a fly on the wall, fly on the wall, fly on the wall!" (*Exeunt, with arms linked.*)

SCENE TWO
A ROOM

KING PETER *is being dressed by two* VALETS.

PETER: (*While he is being dressed.*) Men must think, and I have to think for my subjects, for they don't think, they don't think at all.—The substance is the thing in itself, and that's myself. (*He runs around the room, almost naked.*) Did you get that? *Per se* is the thing in itself, do you understand? Now we need my attributes, modifications, characteristics and accidences: where's my shirt, where are my trousers? —stop! Shame on it! You've left my free will quite exposed in front. Where's morality—where are my cuffs? The categories are in a shocking state of confusion: you've done up two buttons too many, you've put my snuffbox in the right-hand pocket: my whole system has been ruined.—Ha, what's the meaning of this knot in my handkerchief? Hey, there, fellow, what's the meaning of this knot; what was it I wanted to remember?

FIRST VALET: When Your Majesty deigned to tie that knot in your handkerchief you wanted to . . .

PETER: Well?

FIRST VALET: Remind yourself of something.

PETER: An intricate reply. Well, what's your meaning, man?

SECOND VALET: Your Majesty wanted to remind yourself of something when you deigned to tie that knot in your handkerchief.

PETER: (*Runs up and down.*) What? What? These men bewilder me, I'm in the utmost confusion. I simply don't know what to do. (*Enter a* SERVANT.)

SERVANT: Your Majesty, the Cabinet is assembled.

PETER: (*Joyfully.*) Yes, that's it, that's it: I wanted to remind myself of my people. Come on, gentlemen! Walk sym-

metrically. Isn't it very hot? Take your handkerchiefs and
wipe your faces. I am always so embarrassed when I have to
speak in public. (*All go off. Re-enter* KING PETER, *the*
CABINET.) My dear and loyal subjects, herewith I wish to
inform and advise you, inform and advise you—for either
my son marries or he doesn't. (*He puts one finger to his nose.*)
Either, or—you understand, don't you? There is no third
course. Men must think. (*Stands there for some time,
meditating.*) When I speak so loud I don't know who is in
fact speaking, myself or another man; this worries me. (*After
long meditation.*) I am I.—What do you think of that,
President?

PRESIDENT: (*Gravely and slowly.*) Your Majesty, perhaps it is
so, but, on the other hand, perhaps it is not so.

CABINET: (*In chorus.*) Yes, perhaps it is so, but, on the other
hand, perhaps it is not so.

PETER: (*With emotion.*) O my wise Councillors!—Well,
what, in fact, were we talking about? What was it I wanted
to tell you? President, why have you such a faulty memory
on such a solemn occasion? The meeting is adjourned. (*He
retires solemnly, followed by the whole* CABINET.)

SCENE THREE
A LUXURIOUS ROOM. LIGHTED CANDLES

LEONCE *with several* SERVANTS.

LEONCE: Are all the shutters closed? Light the candles.
Enough of daylight! I want night, deep, ambrosial night.
Cover the lamps with crystal bowls and set them between
the oleander trees, so that they'll peer out dreamily like a
girl's eyes under eyelids of leaves. Move the roses closer to
me, so that the wine will fall on their calyces like dew drops.
Music! Where are the violins? Where's Rosetta?—Away
with you! Leave me, all of you! (*Enter* ROSETTA *prettily
dressed. Distant music.*)

ROSETTA: (*Approaches coquettishly.*) Leonce!

LEONCE: Rosetta!

ROSETTA: Leonce!

LEONCE: Rosetta!

ROSETTA: Your lips are weary. With kissing?

LEONCE: With yawning.

ROSETTA: Oh!

LEONCE: Ah, Rosetta, mine is the terrible labor . . .

ROSETTA: Well?

LEONCE: Of doing nothing . . .

ROSETTA: But make love?

LEONCE: That would be labor indeed.

ROSETTA: (*Offended.*) Leonce!

LEONCE: Or a pastime.

ROSETTA: Or idleness.

LEONCE: You're right, as usual. You're a clever girl, and I think highly of your wit.

ROSETTA: So you love me out of boredom?

LEONCE: No, I'm bored because I love you. But I love my boredom as I love you. The two of you are inseparable. *O dolce far niente!* I dream over your eyes as over the marvelous hidden deeps of pools; the caresses of your lips lull me to sleep like the rippling of their little waves. (*He puts his arm around her.*) Come, dear boredom, your kisses are a voluptuous yawning, and your footsteps are a dainty hiatus.

ROSETTA: Do you love me, Leonce?

LEONCE: Why not?

ROSETTA: For ever?

LEONCE: That's a very long word: ever! If I love you only for another five thousand years and seven months, isn't that enough? Of course, it's much less than for ever, but it's still a pretty good stretch, and we can take our time over loving each other.

ROSETTA: Or time can take our love and kill it.

LEONCE: Or our love kill time. Dance, Rosetta, dance, so that time will keep the measure of your pretty feet.

ROSETTA: My feet would rather go right out of time. (*She dances and sings.*)

> O my weary feet, you must be dancing
> in bright shoes dressed
> when rather down below
> in earth you'd rest.

O my hot cheeks, you must be glowing
in love's wild poses,
when rather you'd be blowing
two deep red roses.

O my poor eyes, you must be flashing
in candlelight
when rather you would dull your pain
in endless night.

LEONCE: (*Dreamily.*) Oh, a dying love is more beautiful than a growing one. I'm a Roman; at the lavish feast, for dessert the golden fishes play in their dying colors. How the red glow fades from her cheeks, how slowly her eyes lose their brightness, how lightly the waves of her limbs rise and fall. Adieu, adieu, my love, I shall love your dead body. (ROSETTA *goes up to him again.*) Tears, Rosetta? A fine epicureanism —to be able to weep. Go out and stand in the sun so that these precious drops may crystallize—they should turn into splendid diamonds. You can have them made into a necklace.

ROSETTA: Yes, diamonds indeed, they're cutting into my eyes. Oh Leonce! (*Wants to embrace him.*)

LEONCE: Careful! My head! I've laid out my love inside it. Look in through the windows of my eyes. Can you see how beautifully dead the poor thing is? Can you see the two white roses on its cheeks and the two red ones on its breast? Don't jolt me, or one of its little arms might break off, and that would be a pity. I have to carry my head straight on my shoulders, as the bearer carries a child's coffin.

ROSETTA: (*Jokingly.*) Clown!

LEONCE: Rosetta! (*Rosetta makes a face at him.*) Thank God! (*Covers his eyes.*)

ROSETTA: (*Frightened.*) Leonce, look at me!

LEONCE: Not for anything!

ROSETTA: Just one glance.

LEONCE: Not a single one. What can you be thinking of: just a tiny change and my love would come alive again. I'm glad to have buried it. I'm holding on to the impression.

ROSETTA: (*Exit, sadly and slowly, singing as she goes.*)
        I am a poor little orphan
        I'm afraid to be left alone.
        Oh, dearest grief,
        Won't you come with me to my home?

LEONCE: (*Alone.*) A strange thing, love. Every night for a whole year you lie in bed, half conscious, half asleep, and one fine morning you wake up, drink a glass of water, put on your clothes, pass your hand over your forehead, and look for your bearings—and look for your bearings.—My God, how many women you need to sing the whole scale of love, up and down. One woman hardly covers a note. Why is the mist on our earth a prism that the white-hot ray of love breaks up into a rainbow? (*He drinks.*) In what bottle shall I find the wine for today's drunkenness? Or is the effort beyond me now? It's as though I were sitting under an air pump. The air so sharp and rarefied that I'm freezing—it's like going ice-skating in a pair of nankeen trousers—Gentlemen, gentlemen, do you really know what sort of men Caligula and Nero were? I do.—Come on, Leonce, let's have a soliloquy, I'll listen to you. My life yawns at me like a vast sheet of white paper that I've got to cover with writing, but I can't produce a single letter. My head is an empty ballroom with a few wilted roses and creased ribbons on the floor, violins with broken strings in the corner; the last dancers have taken off their masks and look at one another with eyes weary to the point of death. Twenty-four times a day I turn myself inside out like a glove. Oh, I know myself, I know what I'll be thinking and dreaming in a quarter of an hour's time, in a week's time, in a year's. God, what have I done, why do you make me repeat the same lesson like a schoolboy, again and again? Bravo, Leonce, bravo! (*He claps.*) It makes me feel quite a bit better, to call out to myself like that. Hey, Leonce! Leonce!

VALERIO: (*Emerging from under a table.*) Your Highness, you really seem to have found the right way to the madhouse.

LEONCE: Yes, now that you've pointed it out, I'm inclined to agree with you.

VALERIO: Hold on, we'll discuss the matter at greater length in a minute. I've only got to eat up a chunk of roast meat that I stole from the kitchen and drink up some wine that I stole from your table. I'm almost ready.

LEONCE: How he smacks his lips; the fellow gives me the most idyllic sensations; I could start again with the simplest things, I could eat cheese, drink beer, smoke tobacco. Carry on, but don't grunt so much through your snout and don't munch so hard with your fangs.

VALERIO: Most worthy Adonis, do you fear for your thighs? Don't worry. I'm neither a maker of brooms nor a schoolmaster; I need no twigs for a birch.

LEONCE: You're certainly never at a loss for an answer.

VALERIO: I wish I could say the same of my master.

LEONCE: So that you'll get your thrashing—is that what you mean? Are you so eager to make up for your lack of breeding?

VALERIO: Oh heavens, it's easier to breed than to be well bred. It's sad to reflect how many unhappy events can result from a happy event. How often I've been confined since my mother's confinement. How many bad receptions I owe to my conception!

LEONCE: As far as those conceits are concerned, they couldn't concern me less. Choose your expressions more carefully or my depression will make a most unpleasant impression on you.

VALERIO: When my mother was in the Straits after circumnavigating the Cape of Good Hope . . .

LEONCE: And your father suffered shipwreck on Cape Horn . . .

VALERIO: Quite right; he was a night watchman. Yet he didn't put the horn to his lips as often as the fathers of noble sons put it to their foreheads.

LEONCE: Man, your impudence is sublime. I feel a certain urge to come into close contact with it. I have a strong desire to thrash you.

VALERIO: That's a striking reply and a trenchant corroboration.

LEONCE: (*Goes for him.*) More striking than you think: for you'll get a thrashing for answering back.

VALERIO: (*Runs away.* LEONCE *trips up and falls.*) And you're a corroboration that has yet to be established; for it trips up over its own legs, which, fundamentally, require corroboration themselves. They're a most implausible pair of calves and a most problematic pair of thighs. (*Enter the* CABINET. LEONCE *remains sitting on the floor.* VALERIO.)

PRESIDENT: Your Highness will forgive me . . .

LEONCE: As I forgive myself. As I forgive myself! I forgive myself the kindness of listening to you. Gentlemen, won't you take your places?—How these people make faces when they hear the word "place." Just sit down on the ground and make yourselves at home. After all, it's the last place you'll occupy, though it yields no one any profit—except the gravedigger.

PRESIDENT: (*Embarrassed, snapping his fingers.*) With Your Highness's permission . . .

LEONCE: But don't snap your fingers like that, unless you want to turn me into a murderer.

PRESIDENT: (*Snapping his fingers more loudly.*) Would Your Highness deign, considering . . .

LEONCE: My God, why don't you hide your hands in your trousers or sit on them? The man's quite lost his head. Pull yourself together.

VALERIO: You should never interrupt children when they're pissing, or they'll get inhibited.

LEONCE: Try to collect yourself, man. Think of your family and the State. You're in danger of having a stroke, if your speech recoils on itself.

PRESIDENT: (*Produces a piece of paper from his pocket.*) Your Highness, kindly permit . . .

LEONCE: What? You've learned to read already? All right, then . . .

PRESIDENT: That the awaited arrival of Your Highness' affianced bride, the most gracious Princess Lena of Pipi, is expected tomorrow, thereof his Royal Majesty wishes to inform Your Highness.

LEONCE: If my fiancee is awaiting me, I'll do her the favor of letting her wait for me. I saw her in a dream last night; she had a pair of eyes so large that the dancing shoes of my Rosetta would have fitted over them as eyebrows and on her cheeks there were no dimples but a couple of ditches to drain away laughter. I believe in dreams. Do you ever dream, President? Do you ever have premonitions?

VALERIO: That goes without saying. Always the night before the day a joint is burnt, a capon cops it, or His Royal Majesty gets the stomach-ache.

LEONCE: By the way, weren't you about to say something? Let's have it then; out with it.

PRESIDENT: On the day of the wedding the supreme will of His Royal Majesty is disposed to relegate the most supreme utterances of His will to the hands of Your Highness.

LEONCE: Tell the supreme will that I shall do everything with the exception of what I shall refrain from doing, which, in any case will not be as much as it would be if it were as much again.—Gentlemen, you'll excuse my not showing you out . . . it so happens that I passionately desire to sit down, but my graciousness is so great that I can hardly take its measure with my legs. (*He spreads his legs.*) President, measure the distance, so that you can remind me of it later. Valerio, escort the gentlemen.

VALERIO: Exhort them? Shall I encourage the Lord President with a stick? Shall I drive them out, as if they walked on all fours?

LEONCE: Man, you're nothing more than a bad pun. You have neither father nor mother, but vowels and consonants engendered you between them.

VALERIO: And you, Prince, are a book without letters, with nothing but dashes in it. Come along now, gentlemen. It's a sad thing the word "come." If you want an income, you have to steal; all your efforts to obtain promotion will come to nothing, unless you get yourself hanged; no one will give you a welcome, until you're buried; and the outcome of it is that you're at a loss for another word, as I am, because I can think of nothing more to say, and as you are, before you've said anything at all. We've all witnessed your comedown, gentlemen, and now there's nothing left for you to do but to come away. (*Exeunt* VALERIO *and* ROYAL COUNCIL.)

LEONCE: How vulgarly I played the cavalier with those poor devils! But there's no denying it: there's a certain satisfaction to be derived from a certain kind of vulgarity.—Hm, marriage. That means exhausting a deep well. O Shandy, old Shandy, if only someone would give me your clock. (VALERIO *comes back.*) Oh, Valerio, did you hear it?

VALERIO: Well, you're to be king. That's a jolly business. You can drive about in a coach all day and watch the people wear out their hats with raising them. You can turn decent people into good soldiers, till it seems as if there had never been any difference between them. You can turn black frock coats and white stocks into state officials, and when you die all their polished buttons will turn blue, all the bell-ropes will break like threads with so much ringing. Wouldn't that be fun?

LEONCE: Valerio, Valerio! We must be something different. Guess what!

VALERIO: Oh the sciences, the sciences. We'll become learned men. A priori or a posteriori?

LEONCE: As for a priori, that has to be learnt from my father; and everything begins a posteriori: like an old fairy tale: once upon a time!

VALERIO: Then let's be heroes. (*He marches up and down, drumming and trumpeting.*) Bang—bang—bla—bla—bang.

LEONCE: But heroism frays horribly and starts getting hospital fever and can't be maintained without lieutenants and recruits. Spare me all the romantic driveling over Alexander and Napoleon!

VALERIO: Then let's be geniuses.

LEONCE: The nightingale of poetry warbles all day long over our heads, but all that's finest goes down the drain until we pluck out its feathers and dip them in ink or paint.

VALERIO: Then let's become useful members of the community.

LEONCE: I'd sooner hand in my resignation from humanity.

VALERIO: Then let's go to hell.

LEONCE: Oh, hell only exists for the sake of contrast, to make us understand that, after all, there's something to be said for heaven. (*Jumping up.*) Oh Valerio, Valerio, I've got it now. Can't you feel the breeze that wafts from the south? Can't you feel the deep blue, glowing ether that ebbs and flows, the light flashing on golden, sun-drenched soil, on

the holy salt sea, on marble columns and marble bodies?
Great Pan is sleeping, and the brazen figures dream in the
shade above the deeply whispering waves, dream of Vergil's
old magic, of the tarantella and the tambourine, of dark,
wild nights full of masks, torches, and guitars. A lazzaróne!
A lazzaróne! We're going to Italy.

SCENE FOUR
A GARDEN

PRINCESS LENA, *in bridal attire. The* GOVERNESS.

LENA: Yes, now I've got it. All the time I thought of nothing.
Time simply passed, and then suddenly *the day* rose up
before me. I've got the wreath round my hair—and the
bells, the bells! (*She leans back and closes her eyes.*) Look.
I wish the lawn grew over me and the bees flew over me,
humming; look, now I'm all dressed up and there's rosemary
in my hair. Isn't there an old song:
>   In the graveyard let me lie
>   Like an infant in the cradle.
GOVERNESS: Poor child, how pale you are under those flashing
jewels.
LENA: Oh, I could love someone too: why not? We all walk
about so lonely, groping for a hand to support us until we
die and they separate our hands to lay them folded on each
one's breast. But why do they drive a nail through two
hands that never sought each other? What has my poor
hand done to deserve it? (*She draws a ring from her finger.*)
This ring stings me like a viper.
GOVERNESS: But they say he's a regular Don Carlos!
LENA: Yes, but a man . . .
GOVERNESS: Well?
LENA: Whom one wouldn't love. (*She gets up.*) I'm ashamed,
you see.—Tomorrow I shall have been stripped of all scent
and luster. Am I, then, no more than the poor helpless
stream forced to reflect every image that bends over its
untroubled bed? The flowers are free to open and close their

calyces to the morning sun and the evening breeze. Is a
king's daughter less than a flower?

GOVERNESS: (*Weeping.*) Poor little angel. Why, you're like a
lamb that's going to be sacrificed.

LENA: Indeed I am, and the priest is already raising the knife.
—My God, my God, is it true, then, that our own pain is
our only redemption? Is it true, then, that the world is a
crucified savior, the sun his crown of thorns, the stars the
nails in his feet and the spears in his sides?

GOVERNESS: My child, my child! I can't bear to see you in this
state. It can't go on, it's killing you.—Perhaps, who knows?
I've got a little idea. We shall see. Come along, my dear.
(*She leads the* PRINCESS *away.*)

ACT TWO

SCENE ONE
OPEN FIELD. AN INN IN THE BACKGROUND

(*Enter* LEONCE *and* VALERIO, *carrying a pack.*)

VALERIO: (*Groaning.*) My word, Prince, you must admit that
the world's a pretty rambling sort of edifice.

LEONCE: Not in the least! I feel as if I were in a hall of
mirrors; I hardly dare stretch my arms for fear of colliding
with everything, seeing all the pretty shapes in pieces on
the floor and nothing but the bald bare wall around me.

VALERIO: As for me, I'm lost.

LEONCE: That will be a loss to no one, except to the one who
finds you.

VALERIO: The next thing I'll do is to stand in the shade of my
shadow.

LEONCE: The sun's quite evaporating you. Do you see that
lovely cloud up there? It's at least a quarter of you. It looks
down quite contentedly at your grosser material substance.

VALERIO: The cloud would do no harm to your head if it could
be made to fall on it drop by drop—a delicious thought!
We've already walked through a dozen dukedoms, half a
dozen princedoms, and a couple of kingdoms, and that in
the greatest and quite excessive haste, in a half a day—and
why? Because they want you to be king and marry a
beautiful princess. And you're still alive in such a situation.
I can't understand your resignation. I can't understand why
you haven't taken arsenic, climbed up to the battlements of
the highest tower, and put a bullet through your head, to
make completely sure of it.

LEONCE: But Valerio, remember my ideals. I've got the ideal
of a female inside me and must seek her out. She is infinitely
beautiful and infinitely brainless. That makes her beauty
as helpless, as touching, as a newborn child. It's a delightful
contrast; those divinely stupid eyes, that sublimely simple

17

mouth, that sheep-nosed Greek profile, that animated death within an inanimate body.

VALERIO: Well, I'll be damned. We seem to have arrived at another frontier already. This is a country like an onion: nothing but skins, or like boxes one inside another: in the biggest there's nothing but boxes and in the smallest there's nothing at all. (*He throws down his pack.*) Is this pack to be my gravestone then? Look, Prince, I'm growing philosophical—here's an image of human life: I'm dragging this pack through frost and blazing heat till my feet are sore, because in the evening I want to put on a clean shirt, and when evening comes at last, my brow is furrowed, my cheeks hollow, my eyes dimmed, and I've just got time to put on my shirt as a shroud. Wouldn't it have been wiser to have picked up my pack, sold it in the first tavern we came to, got drunk on the proceeds, and slept in the shade till evening, without having to sweat or wear skin off my feet? And now, Prince, we come to the proof and practical application: out of pure modesty, we now want to clothe the inner man as well, to put on tunic and trousers internally. (*They both make for the inn.*) Oh, my dear pack, what a delicious fragrance, what odors of wine and scents of roast meat! Oh, my dear breeches, now you're rooted in the soil and grow green and blossom, and now long, heavy bunches of grapes hang down into my mouth and the cider ferments in the vat. (*They go off. Enter* PRINCESS LENA *and the* GOVERNESS.)

GOVERNESS: It must be an enchanted day; the sun won't go down, and ages seem to have passed since our flight.

LENA: It isn't that, my dear; the flowers I picked when we left the garden have scarcely wilted.

GOVERNESS: And where shall we rest? We haven't come across a single likely place. I can see no convent, no hermit, no shepherd, even.

LENA: Yes, it was all different in our dreams and books behind the garden wall, among our myrtle and oleander.

GOVERNESS: Oh, the world's a repulsive place. As for the wandering son of a king, we'd better dismiss the possibility at once.

LENA: Oh, the world is lovely and vast, endlessly vast. I should like to go on like this for ever, night and day. Nothing stirs. The roseate radiance of flowers moves on these meadows, and the distant mountains lie on the earth like resting clouds.

GOVERNESS: Oh, heavens, what will they say? And yet it's all so gentle and feminine. It's a renunciation. It's like the flight of Saint Ottilia. But we must be looking for lodging: it's getting dark.

LENA: Yes, the plants are folding their feathery leaves for sleep, and the last rays of the sun lull themselves on the grasses like tired dragonflies.

SCENE TWO

AN INN ON A HILL, BY A STREAM; AN EXTENSIVE VIEW. THE GARDEN OF THE INN

VALERIO, LEONCE.

VALERIO: Well, Prince, you can't deny that your breeches have turned into a delicious drink. Aren't your boots flowing down your throat with the greatest ease?

LEONCE: Do you see those old trees, the hedges, the flowers? Every one of them has its own history, a fascinating and magical history. Do you see the aged friendly faces among the vines on the front door? How they sit holding hands, and how they're afraid because they're so old and the world is still so young. Oh, Valerio, and I'm so young, and the world is so old. Sometimes I feel so afraid for myself I could sit down in a corner weeping hot tears out of self-pity.

VALERIO: (*Handing him a glass.*) Take this diving bell and go down into the sea of wine, so that you'll see pearls flash above you. Look how the elves hover over the calyces of the wine blossoms, shod in gold, beating their cymbals.

LEONCE: (*Jumping up.*) Come on, Valerio, we must do something! We'll occupy ourselves with deep thoughts, we'll examine how it comes about that a chair can stand on three legs but not on two. Come on, we'll pull ants to pieces and count grains of dust. I'll succeed yet in acquiring some princely fad: I'll succeed yet in finding a hobbyhorse to ride until my hands cannot hold the reins and my legs slip out of the stirrups. I've still got a certain dose of enthusiasm to use up; but when I've thoroughly cooked everything, then I need illimitable time to find a spoon with which to eat the dish—and meanwhile it turns stale.

VALERIO: *Ergo bibamus!* This bottle is no lover, no idea, it causes no birth pangs, it never grows tedious, is never unfaithful, it remains true to itself from the first day to the last. You simply break the seal, and all the dreams that lie latent within it bubble out at you.

LEONCE: Oh, God! One half of my life shall be devoted to prayer if only I'm granted a blade of straw on which I may ride as on a noble steed, until I myself lie on the straw.— What an uncanny evening! Down there everything is still, and up there the clouds change and pass, the sunshine goes off and returns. Look at the strange shapes chasing one another over there. Look at the long white shadows with their horribly skinny legs and bat's wings! And it's all so swift, so confused, while down below not a leaf, not a blade of grass, is stirring. The earth has curled up fearfully like a child and over its cradle the spirits walk.

VALERIO: I don't know what's wrong with you; I'm feeling quite comfortable. The sun looks like the sign over an inn and the fiery clouds above it like the inscription: "The Golden Sun." The earth and water down below are like a table on which wine has been spilt, and we're lying on it like playing cards with which God and Satan are having a game out of boredom; you're the king, and I'm the knave, all we need is a queen, a lovely queen, with a big gingerbread heart on her breast and an enormous tulip in which her long nose is drowning sentimentally—(*Enter the* GOVERNESS *and* PRINCESS LENA.) And there she is, by Jove! But it's not really a tulip but a pinch of snuff, and it's not really a nose, but a proboscis. (*To the* GOVERNESS.) Why, most worthy lady, do you walk so fast that one can see your late-lamented calves right to your respectable garters!

GOVERNESS: (*Very angry, stops.*) Why, most honorable gentleman, do you open your mouth so wide that you make a gap in the scenery?

VALERIO: So that, most honorable lady, you won't damage

your nose on the horizon. Such a nose is like the tower of
Lebanon, which looked toward Damascus.

LENA: (*To the* GOVERNESS.) Is the way so long then, my dear?

LEONCE: (*Daydreaming.*) Oh, every way is long. The ticking
of the deathwatch in our breasts is slow, and every drop of
blood takes its time, and our life is a creeping fever. For
tired feet every way is too long.

LENA: (*Who has been listening to him, anxious and pensive.*) And
for tired eyes every kind of light is too sharp, and for tired lips
every breath is too hard (*Smiling.*) and for tired ears every
word is too much. (*She enters the inn with the* GOVERNESS.)

LEONCE: Oh, my dear Valerio! Couldn't I say too: "Would
not this and a forest of feathers with two provincial roses
on my razed shoes get me a cry in a fellowship of players?"
I think I've said it quite melancholically. Thank God I'm
beginning to be delivered of melancholy. The air's no
longer so bright and cold, the sky descends, glowing, close
to me, and wraps me up, and heavy drops are falling—oh
that voice, Valerio: is the way so long then? So many
voices talk on the earth, and we think that they're talking
of other things, but I've understood *this* one. It rests on my
senses like the spirit that hovered over the waters before
there was light. What a ferment in the deeps, what a
growing within me, how that voice is diffused in space!
Is the way so long, then? (*Exit.*)

VALERIO: No, the way to the madhouse is not so long; it's
easily found, I know every footpath, every highway and
byway, that leads to it. I can already see him on his way to
it on a wide avenue, some freezing winter day, his hat under
one arm: I can see him stand in the long shadows of bare
trees fanning himself with his handkerchief.—He's mad as
a coot. (*Follows* LEONCE.)

SCENE THREE
A ROOM

LENA *and the* GOVERNESS.

GOVERNESS: Don't give the man a thought.

LENA: He was so old with all his fair curls. Spring on his

cheeks and winter in his heart. That's sad. A weary body finds its pillow anywhere; but when the spirit is weary, where shall it rest? A horrifying thought has occurred to me: I think there are people who're unhappy, incurably so, only because they *exist*. (*She gets up.*)

GOVERNESS: Where are you going, child?

LENA: I want to go down to the garden.

GOVERNESS: But . . .

LENA: There's no "but" about it, my dear. You know, they should really have planted me in a flower pot. I need the dew and the night air like flowers. Do you hear the harmonies of night? How the crickets sing the day to rest, and the violets lull us to sleep with their scent. I can't stay indoors. The walls are smothering me.

SCENE FOUR
THE GARDEN. NIGHT AND MOONLIGHT

LENA *is seen sitting on the lawn.*

VALERIO: (*Some distance away.*) Nature's a fine thing, but it would be finer still if there were no mosquitoes, if the beds in inns were a little cleaner, and the deathwatch didn't tick so noisily inside the walls. Inside, the people snore and outside the frogs croak; inside, the house crickets chirp and outside the field crickets. Dear lawn, this is a laudable decision. (*Lies down on the lawn.*)

LEONCE: (*Enters.*) O night, ambrosial as the first that descended on Paradise! (*He catches sight of the* PRINCESS *and approaches her softly.*)

LENA: (*Talks to herself.*) The white-throat has twittered in its dreams. The night sleeps more deeply, its cheek grows paler and its breath more soft. The moon's like a sleeping child, its golden curls have strayed into its dear face as it slept. Oh, its sleep is death. How the dead angel rests on his dark pillow, and the stars like candles burn around it. Poor child! It's pitiful—dead and quite alone.

LEONCE: Stand up in your white dress and follow the corpse through the night; sing a requiem for it.

LENA: Who speaks there?

LEONCE: A dream.

LENA: Dreams are blissful.

LEONCE: Then dream yourself blissful, and let me be your dream.

LENA: Death is the most blissful of all dreams.

LEONCE: Then let me be your angel of death. Let my lips graze your eyes like his wings. (*He kisses her.*) Lovely corpse, you rest so beautifully on the black pall of night that nature hates life and falls in love with death.

LENA: No, leave me alone. (*She jumps up and walks away quickly.*)

LEONCE: It's too much! It's too much! My whole being is concentrated in this one moment. Now die! More there could never be. How freshly breathing, gleaming with beauty, creation surges towards me out of chaos. The earth is a bowl made of dark gold: how the light sparkles and froths within it, overflowing the brim; how brightly the stars bubble out like pearls. This one drop of bliss has changed me into a precious vessel. Now away with you, sacred cup! (*He attempts to throw himself into the river.*)

VALERIO: (*Jumps up and clasps him.*) Stop, Your Royal Highness!

LEONCE: Let me go!

VALERIO: I'll let you go as soon as you find a different outlet for your feelings and promise to let the water be.

LEONCE: Ass!

VALERIO: Your Highness, haven't you got over the kind of romanticism you expect of first lieutenants who throw their glasses out of the window after using them to drink the health of their mistresses?

LEONCE: I half-believe you're right.

VALERIO: Console yourself. Even if tonight you don't sleep under the grass, you'll at least sleep on it. It would be quite as suicidal to attempt sleeping in one of those beds. You lie on the straw like a dead man and get bitten by the fleas like a live one.

LEONCE: All right then. (*He lies down on the grass.*)

LEONCE: Man, you've done me out of the most beautiful suicide! If I live to be a hundred, I'll never find such an

excellent moment for it; and the weather couldn't be better.
Now I'm out of the mood already. The fellow has spoilt it
all with his yellow waistcoat and his sky-blue breeches.—
Heaven grant me some really sound and leaden sleep!

VALERIO: Amen.—As for me, I've saved a human life, and my
clear conscience will keep my stomach warm tonight.

LEONCE: May you thrive on it, Valerio.

ACT THREE

SCENE ONE

LEONCE. VALERIO

VALERIO: Get married? Since when, Your Highness, have you been considering the irreparable act?

LEONCE: Do you know, Valerio, that even the least of us is so great that life is still far too short to be able to love him? And then there is a certain class of people who think that there's nothing so good or holy in the world but they must make it still better and holier; they're welcome to their pleasure. There's a certain satisfaction to be derived from this precious arrogance. Why should I grudge them the satisfaction?

VALERIO: Very humanely and philobestially spoken! But does she know who you are?

LEONCE: She only knows that she loves me.

VALERIO: And does Your Highness know who she is?

LEONCE: Idiot! Go and ask the carnation and the columbine for their names.

VALERIO: That means she is something at least, unless even that is too indelicate and smacks of the record files. Yes, but how's it going to work out? Tell me, Prince, shall I be Prime Minister if today your father welds you to the unspeakable, the nameless, by means of the marriage ceremony?

LEONCE: My word on it!

VALERIO: The poor devil Valerio presents his compliments to His Excellency the Prime Minister, the Lord Valerio of Valeriano.—"What does this fellow want? I don't know him. Off with you, rascal!" (*He runs away.* LEONCE *follows him.*)

SCENE TWO

AN OPEN PLACE IN FRONT OF KING PETER'S PALACE

RURAL COUNCILLOR. SCHOOLMASTER. PEASANTS *in their
Sunday-best carrying branches of pine trees.*

RURAL C: Tell me, dear schoolmaster, is the bearing of your
men satisfactory?

SCHOOLMASTER: They're bearing up so well in their sufferings
that for some time they've been bearing with each other.
They're pouring liquor down their gullets most conscienti-
ously, else they couldn't possibly bear the heat for so long.
Take courage, my good fellows! Hold your pine branches
straight in front of you, so that people will think you're a
pine wood, and your noses the wild strawberries, and your
three-cornered hats the antlers of deer, and your leather
breeches the moonlight in it. And remember: the man at
the back must keep running to the front, so that it will look
as if you'd been squared.

RURAL C: And you, Schoolmaster, stand for sobriety.

SCHOOLMASTER: Evidently, for I can hardly stand up, I'm so
sober.

RURAL C: Attention, men! In the program it says: "All the
King's subjects, without exception, will voluntarily line up
on the roadside, neatly dressed, well-nourished, and with a
contented look on their faces." Don't disgrace us.

SCHOOLMASTER: Bear up! Don't scratch yourselves behind the
ears and don't blow your noses as the royal couple drives
past, and show the appropriate emotion, or we shall resort
to the most emotive means to make you. Appreciate what
has been done for you: you've been placed in exactly the
right position for the breeze from the kitchen to waft over
you; you'll be able to smell roast meat for once in your lives.
Do you know your lines? Eh? *Vi!*

THE PEASANTS: *Vi!*

SCHOOLMASTER: *Vat!*

THE PEASANTS: *Vat!*

SCHOOLMASTER: *Vivat!*

THE PEASANTS: *Vivat!*

SCHOOLMASTER: There you are, sir. You see how intelligence

is on the increase. After all, it's Latin. Also tonight we're having a transparent dance on the strength of the holes in our jackets and trousers, and we'll plant rosettes on one another's heads with our fists.

SCENE THREE
A LARGE HALL

LADIES *and* GENTLEMEN, *elegantly dressed, in tidy groups. The* MAJORDOMO *and several* SERVANTS *in the foreground.*

MAJORDOMO: It's a crying shame. Everything is being ruined. The roast is drying up. All the congratulations are turning stale. All the stand-up collars are flopping down like melancholy sows' ears. The peasants' nails and beards are growing again. The soldiers' curls are coming undone. Of all the twelve bridesmaids, there isn't one who wouldn't prefer the horizontal posture to the vertical one.

FIRST SERVANT: In their white gowns they look like exhausted angora rabbits, and the poet laureate grunts around them like a solicitous guinea pig. The commissioned officers are losing all their military bearing, and the ladies-in-waiting stand about like the leaning tower of Pisa. The salt is crystallizing on their necklaces.

SECOND SERVANT: You at least are taking it easy—one couldn't complain that there's a burden on your shoulders. Even if you never unbutton your heart, your shirt at least is unbuttoned down to your heart.

MAJORDOMO: Yes, they're excellent maps of the Turkish Empire—you can find the Dardanelles and the Sea of Marmara. Get on with your work, you knaves. To the windows! There comes His Majesty! (*Enter* KING PETER *and the* CABINET.)

PETER: So the Princess too has vanished. Is there no trace of our beloved son and heir? Have my orders been obeyed? Are the frontiers being watched?

MAJORDOMO: Yes, Your Majesty. The view from this hall permits the strictest surveillance. (*To* FIRST SERVANT.) What did you see?

FIRST SERVANT: A dog looking for its master has run through the kingdom.

MAJORDOMO: (*To the others.*) And you?

SECOND SERVANT: There's someone going for a walk on the north frontier, but it isn't the Prince, I'd recognize him.

MAJORDOMO: And you?

THIRD SERVANT: Begging your pardon, sir, nothing.

MAJORDOMO: That's very little. And you?

FOURTH SERVANT: Nothing, either.

MAJORDOMO: That's just about as much.

PETER: But, members of the Cabinet, did I not resolve that My Royal Majesty should rejoice and that the wedding should be celebrated? Was not that our most solemn resolution?

PRESIDENT: Yes, Your Majesty, thus it has been recorded and set down.

PETER: And should I not compromise myself if I did not carry out my resolution?

PRESIDENT: If it were in any way possible for Your Majesty to compromise yourself, this would be a case in which you might do so.

PETER: Have I not pledged my royal word?—Yes, I shall immediately carry out my resolution: I shall proceed to rejoice. (*He rubs his hands.*) Oh, I'm quite extraordinarily joyful!

PRESIDENT: We all share the feelings of Your Majesty as far as it is fit and possible for your subjects to do so.

PETER: Oh, I simply don't know what to do, I'm so full of joy. I shall have red tunics made for my gentlemen-in-waiting, I shall promote several cadets to lieutenants, I shall allow my subjects—yes, but what about the wedding? Does not the other half of the resolution lay down that the wedding shall be celebrated?

PRESIDENT: It does, Your Majesty.

PETER: Yes, but if the Prince does not come, nor the Princess either?

PRESIDENT: Yes, if the Prince does not come, nor the Princess either—then—then—

PETER: Then what?

PRESIDENT: Then they simply cannot get married.

PETER: Stop! Is the conclusion logical? If—then—Quite right. But my word, my royal word?

PRESIDENT: May Your Majesty take comfort from other majesties. A royal word is a thing—a thing—a thing—that's nothing—

PETER: (*To* THE SERVANTS.) Do you still see nothing?

THE SERVANTS: Nothing, Your Majesty, nothing at all.

PETER: Just when I'd resolved to be so joyful! I was going to begin on the stroke of noon and rejoice for no less than twelve hours—I'm growing quite melancholy.

PRESIDENT: All subjects are requested to share His Majesty's feelings.

MAJORDOMO: To those, however, who have no handkerchiefs weeping is forbidden on grounds of decency.

FIRST SERVANT: Just a minute! I can see something. It's something like a projection, like a nose, but the rest hasn't yet crossed the frontier; and then I can see a man, and two more persons of the opposite sex.

MAJORDOMO: In which direction?

FIRST SERVANT: They're coming closer. They're making for the palace. Here they are. (*Enter* VALERIO, LEONCE, *the* GOVERNESS, *and the* PRINCESS *masked.*)

PETER: Who are you?

VALERIO: How should I know? (*He slowly takes off several masks, one after the other.*) Am I this? Or this? Or this? Really, I'm almost afraid that I shall go on peeling and skinning myself till there's nothing left.

PETER: (*Perplexed.*) But—you must be *something*?

VALERIO: Yes, if that's Your Majesty's command. But in that case, gentlemen, turn the mirrors to the wall and hide your polished buttons, and don't look at me so that I have to see my reflection in your eyes, or I shall really no longer know who I am.

PETER: The man plunges me into perplexity; he exasperates me. I'm in the utmost confusion.

VALERIO: But in actual fact I wished to announce to the exalted and highly esteemed company the arrival here of the two world-famous automatons, of which two I am perhaps the third and the most remarkable—that is, if I myself were really sure who I am, which in fact is not a thing to be wondered at because I myself know nothing about what I'm saying to you, nor indeed know that I don't know it, so that most probably they're only *making* me talk and it's nothing more than cogs and airpipes that are saying all this. (*In a mechanical, rattling tone of voice.*) Ladies and gentlemen, you have here two persons of either sex, a male and a female, a gentleman and a lady. Nothing but artifice and mechanism, nothing but cardboard and watch springs! Each of them has a very sensitive, very sensitive ruby spring beneath the nail of the little toe of the right foot; you press it a little and the machinery runs for no less than fifty years. These persons are of such perfect workmanship that they would be quite indistinguishable from other people if one didn't know that they're mere cardboard; they could easily be turned into members of human society. They're very aristocratic, for they speak with the right accent. They're very moral, for they get up on the stroke of the clock, have lunch on the stroke of the clock, and go to bed on the stroke of the clock; also they have a good digestion, which proves they've got a clear conscience. They have a fine sense of decency, for the lady has no words for the concept of trousers and, as for the man, it's quite impossible for him to walk up the stairs behind a lady or to walk down them in front of one. They're highly educated, for the lady sings all the latest operas and the gentleman wears cuffs.— Attention, ladies and gentlemen, they're now at an interesting stage: the mechanism of love is beginning to function; the gentleman has already once carried the lady's wrap, the lady has already once rolled her eyes and raised them to heaven. Both have whispered more than once: faith, hope, and charity! Both already look perfectly synchronized; they need nothing more but the tiny word: Amen.

PETER: (*Thinking hard.*) In effigy? In effigy? President, if one hangs a man in effigy, isn't that just as good as to hang him properly?

PRESIDENT: Begging Your Majesty's pardon, it's even better, much better, for he suffers no harm by it and yet he's hanged all the same.

PETER: Now I've got it. We shall celebrate the wedding in effigy. (*Pointing at* LEONCE *and* LENA.) That's the Princess, that's the Prince.—I shall carry out my resolution, and I shall rejoice.—Let the bells peal! Get your congratulations ready, quickly, Court Chaplain. (*The* COURT CHAPLAIN *steps forward, clears his throat, raises his eyes to heaven several times.*)

VALERIO: Begin! Leave thy damnable faces and begin. Good luck!

COURT CHAPLAIN: (*In the utmost confusion.*) When we—or—but.

VALERIO: Henceforth and notwithstanding.

COURT CHAPLAIN: For—

VALERIO: It was before the creation of the world.

COURT CHAPLAIN: That—

VALERIO: God was bored.

PETER: Make it brief, my good fellow.

COURT CHAPLAIN: (*Regaining his composure.*) If Your Highness, Prince Leonce of the kingdom of Popo, agree, and if Your Highness, Princess Lena of the kingdom of Pipi, agree, and if your Highnesses agree mutually to have the other reciprocally, then pronounce a clear and audible "Yes."

LEONCE and LENA: Yes.

COURT CHAPLAIN: Then I say "Amen."

VALERIO: Excellently done, briefly and to the point; well, that's that: man and woman have been created, and all the beasts of Paradise surround them. (LEONCE *takes off his mask.*)

ALL: The Prince!

PETER: The Prince! My son! I am lost. I am deceived! (*He makes for the* PRINCESS.) Who is this person? The whole ceremony is declared invalid herewith.

GOVERNESS: (*Takes off the* PRINCESS'S *mask triumphantly.*)

LEONCE: Lena?

LENA: Leonce?

LEONCE: Oh, Lena, I think this was the flight *into* Paradise.

LENA: I'm deceived.

LEONCE: I'm deceived.

LENA: O chance!

LEONCE: O Providence.

VALERIO: I can't help laughing. It's to an accident without precedent that Your Highnesses owe your present predicament. I hope that you'll cement the accident by being content with each other. So much for the incident!

GOVERNESS: Ah, to think that my old eyes have survived to see this! The wandering son of a king! Now I shall die at peace.

PETER: My children. I am moved, I scarcely know what to do, I am so moved. I am the happiest of men. I must add that herewith I most solemnly entrust the government of this kingdom to you, my son, and shall immediately proceed to think undisturbed. My son, you will leave these wise men to me (*Pointing to the* CABINET) so that they may support me in my endeavors. Come along, gentlemen, we must think, think undisturbed. (*Exit with* CABINET.) Just now that fellow plunged me into perplexity; I must find my way out of it.

LEONCE: (*To all those present.*) Gentlemen, my consort and I infinitely regret your long attendance today. Your position is so pitiable that on no account do we wish to prolong this trial of your patience. Go home now, but don't forget your speeches, sermons, and verses, for tomorrow the fun will begin all over again, though at your leisure and convenience. Good-bye! (*Exeunt all, except* LEONCE, LENA, VALERIO, *and the* GOVERNESS.) Well, Lena, don't you see now that all our pockets are full of puppets and toys? What shall we do with them? Shall we paint mustaches on them and buckle swords to their belts? Or shall we dress them in tailcoats, have them occupy themselves with infusorian politics and diplomacy while we sit down beside them with a microscope? Or do you long for a barrel organ on which milk-white aesthetic mice may dance about? Shall we build a theater? (LENA *leans against him and shakes her head.*) But I know better what you want: we'll have all the clocks broken, all calendars forbidden, and we'll count hours and moons only by the flowers, by blossom and fruit. And then we'll have the little country surrounded by magnifying mirrors to catch the sun, so that there'll be no more winter, so that in summer we'll distill the climate to the point it reaches in India and Capri and spend the whole year among roses and violets, among oranges and laurel.

VALERIO: And I shall be Prime Minister, and we'll publish a decree that anyone who works till his hands are callused shall be placed in protective custody; that anyone who works himself sick will be guilty of a criminal offense; that anyone who boasts of eating his bread in the sweat of his brow shall be declared mad and dangerous to the community; and then we'll lie down in the shade and pray to God for macaroni, melons, and figs, for musical throats, classical bodies, and a comfortable religion.

LENZ

On the twentieth of January Lenz went across the mountains. The summits and the high slopes covered with snow, gray stones all the way down to the valleys, green plains, rocks, and pine trees.

It was damp and cold; water trickled down the rocks and gushed over the path. The branches of the pine trees drooped heavily in the moist air. Gray clouds traveled in the sky, but all was so dense—and then the mist rose like steam, slow and clammy, climbed through the shrubs, so lazy, so awkward. Indifferently he moved on; the way did not matter to him, up or down. He felt no tiredness, only sometimes it struck him as unpleasant that he could not walk on his head.

At first there was an urge, a movement inside him, when the stones and rocks bounded away, when the gray forest shook itself beneath him and the mist now blurred its outlines, now half-unveiled the trees' gigantic limbs; there was an urge, a movement inside him, he looked for something, as though for lost dreams, but he found nothing. All seemed so small to him, so near, so wet. He would have liked to put the whole earth to dry behind the stove, he could not understand why so much time was needed to descend a steep slope, to reach a distant point; he thought that a few paces should be enough to cover any distance. Only from time to time, when the storm thrust clouds into the valley, and the mist rose in the forest, when the voices near the rocks awoke, now like thunder subsiding far away, now rushing back toward him, as if in their wild rejoicing they desired to sing the praise of earth, and the clouds like wild neighing horses galloped toward him, and the sunbeams pierced in between and came to draw a flashing sword against the snow-covered plains, so that a

bright, dazzling light cut across the summits into the valleys;
or when the gale drove the clouds downward and hurled them
into a pale-blue lake, and then the wind died down and from
the depths of the ravines, from the crests of the pine trees
drifted upward, with a humming like that of lullabies and
pealing bells, and a soft red hue mingled with the deep azure,
and little clouds on silver wings passed across, and everywhere
the mountain tops, sharp and solid, shone and glittered for
miles—then he felt a strain in his chest, he stood struggling
for breath, heaving, his body bent forward, his eyes and mouth
wide open; he thought that he must draw the storm into himself,
contain it all within him, he stretched himself out and lay on
the earth, dug his way into the All, it was an ecstasy that hurt
him—he rested and laid his head in the moss and half-closed
his eyes, and then it withdrew, away, far away from him, the
earth receded from him, became small as a wandering star and
dipped down into a roaring stream that moved its clear waters
beneath him. But these were only moments; then, soberly, he
would rise, resolute, calm, as though a shadow play had passed
before his eyes—he remembered nothing.

Toward evening he came to the highest point of the
mountain range, to the snowfield from which one descended
again into the flat country in the west; he sat down on the top.
It had grown calmer toward evening; the cloud formations,
constant and motionless, hung in the sky; as far as the eyes
could reach, nothing but summits from which broad stretches
of land descended, and everything so still, so gray, lost in
twilight. He experienced a feeling of terrible loneliness; he
was alone, quite alone. He wanted to talk to himself, but he
could not, he hardly dared to breathe; the bending of his feet
sounded like thunder beneath him, he had to sit down. He was
seized with a nameless terror in this nothingness: he was in
the void! He leapt to his feet and rushed down the slope.

It had grown dark, heaven and earth were melting into one.
It seemed as though something were following him, as though
something horrible must catch up with him, something that
men cannot bear, as though madness on horseback were
chasing him.

At last he heard voices; he was relieved, his heart grew

lighter. He was told that another half-hour would see him to Waldbach.

He passed through the village. Lights shone in the windows, he looked inside as he went by: children at table, old women, girls, all with quiet, composed faces. It seemed to him that it was these faces that radiated light; he began to feel quite cheerful, and soon he was at the vicarage in Waldbach.

They were at table when he came in; his blond hair hung in locks about his pale face, his eyes and the corners of his mouth were twitching, his clothes were torn.

Oberlin welcomed him, thinking he was a workman: "You're welcome, although you're a stranger to me."

"I'm a friend of ——'s, and convey his regards to you."

"Your name, if you please?"

"Lenz."

"Ha, ha, ha, has it not appeared in print? Haven't I read several dramas ascribed to a gentleman of that name?"

"Yes, but be kind enough not to judge me by them."

The conversation continued, he groped for words and told his story quickly, but in torment; gradually he was calmed by the homely room and the quiet faces that stood out from the shadows; the bright child's face on which the light seemed to rest and which looked up inquisitively and trustingly, and the mother who sat further back in the shadow, motionless as an angel. He began to tell them about his home; he drew a number of costumes; they surrounded him closely, sympathetically, soon he felt at home. His pale childish face, now smiling, his lively manner when telling his story! He became calm; it seemed to him as though familiar figures, forgotten faces, stepped again from the darkness, old songs awoke, he was away, far away.

At last it was time to go. He was escorted across the street, the vicarage was too small, he was given a room in the schoolhouse. He went upstairs. It was cold up there, a large room, empty, a high bedstead in the background. He put down the light on the table and walked about. He recalled what day it was, how he had come, where he was. The room in the vicarage with its lights, its dear faces; it was like a shadow to him, a dream, and he felt the emptiness again, as he had felt

it on the mountain; but now he could not fill it in with anything, the light had gone out, darkness swallowed everything.
An unspeakable terror possessed him. He leapt to his feet, ran
out of the room, down the stairs, out of the house; but in vain,
all was dark, a nothing—even to himself he was a dream.
Single, isolated thoughts flickered up, he held them fast; he
felt constrained to say "Our Father" again and again. He
could no longer find himself. An obscure instinct urged him
to save himself; he ran into stones, tore himself with nails.
The pain began to recall him to consciousness; he hurled himself into the basin of the fountain, but the water was not deep,
he splashed about.

Then people came; they had heard him, they called out to
him. Oberlin came running out. Lenz had come to his senses,
the full consciousness of his situation returned to him, he felt
more at ease. Now he was ashamed of himself and regretted
that he had frightened the good people; he told them it was
his habit to take a cold bath, and went back to his room. At last
exhaustion gave him rest.

The next day all went well. With Oberlin through the
valley on horseback; vast mountain slopes contracting from
great heights into a narrow winding valley that extended high
up into the mountains in many directions; large masses of rock,
which grew wider at the base, very little wooded country, but
all rising solemn and gray; a view of the west, into the country
and the mountain range that runs from south to north with
mighty peaks that stand grave or silently motionless, like a
dawning dream. Immense masses of light swelling forth from
the valleys at times like a river of gold, and again clouds that
hung beside the highest summits and then drifted slowly down
the forest into the valley, or rose and sank in shafts of sunlight
like a hovering, silvery specter; no noise, no movement, not a
bird, nothing but the now near, now distant flight of the wind.
Also there appeared dots, skeletons of huts, boards covered with
straw, black, earnest in color. The people, taciturn and grave,
as though afraid to disturb the quiet of their valley, greeted
them calmly as they rode by.

Inside the cottages it was lively; everyone crowded around
Oberlin, who instructed, advised, consoled; trusting glances,

prayers everywhere. The people told of dreams, premonitions. Then quickly returned to practical life; paths constructed, channels dug, school attended. Oberlin was indefatigable, Lenz constantly at his side, conversing, attending to business, or submerged in the scenery. All of it had a beneficent, soothing effect upon him. Often he was compelled to look into Oberlin's eyes, and the immense repose communicated to us by nature at rest, in the midst of a forest, in moonlit, melting summer nights, seemed even nearer to him in those calm eyes, those revered, earnest features. He was shy; but he made remarks, he spoke. To Oberlin his conversation gave much pleasure, and Lenz's graceful and childish face delighted him.

But only as long as daylight filled the valley could he endure it; toward evening a strange awe took possession of him, he felt like running after the sun; gradually, as objects became more shadowy, all appeared so dreamlike, so antagonistic to him; he was seized with fear, like children left to sleep in the dark, it seemed to him that he was blind. Now his terror grew, the nightmare of madness sat at his feet, the unalterable thought that all was only a dream opened to him; he clung to every object. Shapes passed swiftly before his eyes, he tried to hold them; they were shadows, the life was drained out of him, his limbs were quite paralyzed. He spoke, he sang, he recited passages from Shakespeare, he clutched at everything that at another time would have made his blood flow more quickly, he tried everything, but cold, cold! He had to go out into the open air. What little light he could see strewn through the night, once his eyes had got used to the darkness, made him feel better; he hurled himself into the basin of the fountain, the stark effect of the water made him feel better; besides, he had secret hopes of an illness—and now he conducted his bathing less noisily.

But as he got used to his new way of life he grew calmer. He assisted Oberlin, sketched, read the Bible; old, discarded hopes reasserted themselves: the New Testament seemed so near to him here . . . When Oberlin told him how an invisible hand had held him back on the bridge, how on the summit a radiance had dazzled his eyes, how he had heard a voice, how it had spoken to him in the night and how God had wholly

entered his heart, so that like a child he would cast dice when-
ever he did not know what to do: this faith, this eternal
Heaven on earth, this being in God—only now Holy Writ
became quite clear to him. How close was nature to the people
here, how close all the heavenly mysteries; yet neither violent
nor majestic, but still familiar.

One morning he went out. It had snowed in the night; now
the valley was filled with bright sunshine, though further
away the landscape was half-veiled in mist. He soon strayed
from the path, up a gentle rise, no more trace of footsteps, a
pine forest on one side; the sun was caught in crystals, the
snow was light and flaky, here and there the track of wild
animals softly imprinted on the snow, leading into the mountains. Not a movement in the air other than a soft breeze or the
faint rustle of a bird shaking snow from its tail. All so still and
far above, the trees with swaying white feathers in the deep-
blue air. Gradually the scene became familiar to him: the
immense, uniform lines and planes, whose aspect sometimes
suggested to him that they were addressing him with mighty
voices, were shrouded; a familiar feeling as of Christmas crept
upon him: sometimes he thought that his mother would step
from behind a tree to tell him that all these were her presents
to him; she would be tall as in those days. As he descended he
saw that a rainbow of rays had gathered around his shadow;
he felt as though something had touched his forehead: the
created world was speaking to him.

He came down. Oberlin was in the room, Lenz went up to
him gaily and told him that perhaps he would deliver a sermon
one day. "Are you a theologian?"—"Yes."—"Good, next
Sunday, then."

Happy, Lenz went up to his room. He was thinking about
a text for a sermon and grew pensive, his nights restful.
Sunday morning came, the thaw had begun. Clouds gliding
past, blue in between. The church stood nearby, up the
mountain, on a projection, round about it the churchyard.
Lenz was standing up above when the bell pealed and the
churchgoers, women and girls in their grave black costumes, a
white folded handkerchief on each hymnbook and a spray of
rosemary, came up or down the narrow paths, between rocks

from various directions. Sometimes a glance of sunshine rested on the valley, the warm air stirred slowly, the landscape swam in a sweet odor, distant ringing of bells—it seemed as if everything were being merged in a single harmonious wave.

In the little churchyard the snow was gone, dark moss beneath black crosses; a belated rosebush leaned against the churchyard wall, belated flowers as well from under the moss; sometimes sunshine, then again darkness. The service began, the human voices met in a pure bright chord; an impression like that of looking into a clean, translucent mountain stream. The singing subsided, Lenz began to speak. He was diffident; under the spell of the music his inner convulsions had ceased, but now his whole agony stirred again and settled in his heart. A sweet sensation of infinite well-being came upon him. With those people he spoke simply, they suffered with him; and it was a comfort to be able to bring sleep to eyes that have wept themselves tired, peace to tormented hearts, to turn heavenward this muted suffering of an existence tormented by material needs. He had become more confident as he concluded —but then the voices struck up again:

"Let the holy pain within me
Release deep wells entirely;
Let suffering be all my gain,
Suffering be my service then."

The urge within him, the music, the agony shattered him. The All seemed full of wounds; he felt deep, unspeakable pain because of it. Now for a different life: divine, twitching lips bent over him and attached themselves to his lips; he returned to his solitary room. He was alone, alone! Then the well gushed forth, streams broke from his eyes, he contorted himself, his limbs convulsed in a spasm, he felt as if he were about to dissolve, the voluptuous crisis seemed interminable. At last it grew dark inside him, he experienced a soft, profound compassion for himself, he wept for himself, his head sank down upon his chest, he went to sleep. A full moon hung in the sky; locks of hair fell on his cheeks—so he lay alone, and all was silent and still and cold, and the moon shone all night and hung above the mountains.

Next morning he came down and told Oberlin quite calmly how in the night his mother had appeared to him: dressed in white, she had stepped from the dark churchyard wall, a red rose and a white rose fastened to her breast; she had sunk down into a corner and slowly the roses had overgrown her— she must surely be dead; he was quite untroubled on that account.

In reply Oberlin described to him how he had been alone in a field at the time of his father's death and had heard a voice, so that he knew his father was dead; and when he went home he found that it was so. This led him to speak of other things, he told Lenz of the people in the mountains, about girls who could feel the presence of water and metal underground, about men who on many a mountaintop had been seized and had wrestled with a spirit; he told him also how once, by gazing into the deep void of a mountain pool, he had fallen into a kind of somnambulism. Lenz said that the spirits of the waters had come upon him, enabling him to feel something of his true nature. He went on: the simplest and purest individuals were most closely related to the elements; the more subtle a man's intellectual life and perceptions, the more blunted this sense of the elemental became; he did not consider it an exalted state of mind, because it was not independent enough, but he thought it must give one a sense of infinite bliss to be thus touched by the individual life of every form of creation, to have a soul that would communicate with stones, metals, water, and plants, as in a dream to absorb into oneself every being in nature, as flowers absorb air according to the waxing and waning of the moon.

He expressed other ideas; how in all things there was an indescribable harmony, a tone, a blissfulness that in the higher forms required a greater number of organs to externalize themselves, to respond, to apprehend, but that consequently these were the more deeply susceptible; while in the lower forms all was more repressed, more limited, but consequently contained more repose. He pursued this farther; Oberlin cut him short, it led him too far from his simple ways. Another time Oberlin showed him some small cakes of paint and explained to him in what manner each color was related to human beings; he produced twelve apostles, each represented by one color. Lenz understood, he spun out the thread even farther, fell into fearful dreams, began, like Stilling,[1] to read the Apocalypse and studied the Bible assiduously.

At about this time Kaufmann[2] and his fiancée came to the Steintal. At first this visit displeased Lenz; he had, as it were, feathered a little nest for himself, and this little bit of peace was so precious to him. And now someone was coming to see him, somebody who reminded him of so much, with whom he must talk and argue, somebody who knew his circumstances. Oberlin knew nothing about his past; he had put him up, looked after him, had regarded his coming as a piece of providence, for it was God who had sent him this unhappy man; he loved Lenz with all his heart. Besides, Lenz's presence was necessary to everyone there; he belonged to them, as if he had long been with them, and no one asked whence he had come and where he would go.

During the meal Lenz recaptured his good mood; they were talking about literature, he was on his own ground. The idealistic movement was just beginning at that time, Kaufmann was one of its supporters. Lenz ardently opposed him. He said: "Even the poets of whom we say that they reproduce reality have no conception of what reality is, but they're a good deal more bearable than those who wish to transform reality." He said: "I take it that God has made the world as it should be and that we can hardly hope to scrawl or daub anything better; our only aspiration should be to re-create modestly in His manner. In all things I demand—life, the possibility of existence, and that's all; nor is it our business to ask whether it's beautiful, whether it's ugly. The feeling that there's life

1. J. H. Jung-Stilling (1740–1817) was a Pietist; the first part of his long autobiographical novel was published by Goethe in 1777; five other volumes followed in the course of his life. (Transl.)

2. Christoph Kaufmann (1753–1795) lived at Winterthur, Switzerland, where Lenz stayed with him for some months. He was the writer of abstruse tracts for the betterment of mankind and a protégé of Lavater's. He had made the acquaintance of Lenz at Weimar in 1776 and visited Lenz's relatives in Livonia during a tour of Europe in the following year. (Transl.)

in the thing created is much more important than considerations of beauty and ugliness; it's the sole criterion in matters of art. Besides, it's only rarely that we find this quality; we find it in Shakespeare; it strikes us with full impact in popular ballads and songs, only sometimes in Goethe; everything else should be thrown on the fire. Those poor wretches aren't capable of drawing as much as a dog's kennel; ideal personages is what they ask for, but all I've seen is a lot of wooden puppets. This idealism is the most shameful contempt for human nature. If only artists would try to submerge themselves in the life of the very humblest person and to reproduce it with all its faint agitations, hints of experience, the subtle, hardly perceptible play of his features . . ." He himself had tried something of the kind in his "Private Tutor" and "The Soldiers." "These are the most prosaic people in the world, but the emotional vein is identical in almost every individual; all that varies is the thickness of the shell that this vein must penetrate. All one needs for these things is eyes and ears in one's head. Yesterday, as I was walking along the edge of the valley, I saw two girls sitting on a stone; one of them was putting up her hair, the other was helping her. Her golden hair hung down; a grave, pale face, and yet so young, and the black dress, and the other one so anxiously busying herself. The finest, most intimate pictures of the German School can hardly give us an idea of what this scene was like. Sometimes one would like to be a Medusa's head, so as to be able to transform such a group into stone and show it to people. The girls got up, destroying this fine composition; yet as they were descending between the rocks a new picture was made. The most beautiful pictures, the richest harmonies group and dissolve. Only one thing remains: an unending loveliness that moves from one form to another, eternally undone, eternally changing. Of course one can't always hold on to it, put it into art galleries or bars of music and then fetch the old and the young, let boys and old men chatter about it and be filled with delight. One must love human nature in order to penetrate into the peculiar character of any individual; nobody, however insignificant, however ugly, should be despised; only then can one understand humankind as a whole. The most undistinguished face can make a deeper impression than the mere perception of abstract beauty, and one can allow one's characters to emerge from one's own mind without copying in any of the externals, without adding details in which one feels no life, no muscles, no pulsations beating in response to one's own."

Kaufmann objected that in the real world he would never find the prototype for an Apollo Belvedere or a Madonna by Raphael. "What does it matter?" Lenz replied; "I must confess that they make me feel quite dead. When I'm in a state of great mental activity they could, perhaps make me feel something, but then I should be doing most of the work. Best of all I like that poet and that visual artist who can reproduce nature for me with the greatest degree of truthfulness, so that I can feel his creation; everything else puts me off. I prefer the Dutch painters to the Italian, because they're the only ones I can grasp. I know only two pictures, and those by Dutch or Flemish painters, that have given me an impression comparable to that of the New Testament: one of them, I don't know who painted it, is Christ and the Disciples at Emmaus. When one reads how the Disciples went forth, the whole of nature is in those few words. It is a dim, twilit evening, a straight red streak of red on the horizon, half dark in the street; then a stranger approaches them, they speak, he breaks bread; then they recognize Him, in a simply human manner, and the divinely suffering features speak to them distinctly, and they are frightened, for it is now dark and something incomprehensible confronts them; but there is nothing ghostly about their fear, it is as though someone we love and who is dead were to approach us at dusk in his old familiar way; that's what the picture is like, with its surface of monotonous brown, the dim, quiet evening. Then there's the other picture: a woman sitting in her room, a prayerbook in her hand. Everything is dressed in its Sunday best, sand has been strewn on the floor, all homely, clean and warm. The woman has been unable to go to church, and she's conducting the service at home: the window is open, she sits inclined toward it, and it seems as if the sound of the village bells were drifting in through the windows, across the wide flat landscape, and the singing of the nearby congregation were reaching her faintly from the church, while the woman looks up the appropriate text."

In this fashion they talked on; the others listened attentively, much of what Lenz said impressed them. He had become flushed as he spoke and, now smiling, now serious, shook his blond locks. He had quite forgotten himself.

After the meal Kaufmann took him aside. He had received letters from Lenz's father, who said his son must go back to assist him. Kaufmann told him that he was idling away his life here, wasting it recklessly, that he should set himself an aim— and more in this strain. Lenz turned on him: "Leave here, leave? Go home? To go mad there? You know I can't bear to live anywhere but in these parts. If I weren't able to go up a mountain at times, to look at the scenery, and then go down again to the house, through the garden, and then look in through the window—I'd go mad, I tell you, mad! Why don't you leave me alone? Just a little peace, now that I'm beginning to feel almost well again. Go away? I don't understand you, those two words make a mess of the world. Everyone needs something; if he's able to rest, what more could he have? What's the use of continually climbing, struggling, eternally throwing away everything the moment gives you, continually suffering so as to enjoy some future state! To be thirsty while a bright spring flows across your path! Here life is bearable to me, and here I'll stay. Why, you ask, why? Simply because that's my will. What does my father want? What can he give me? Impossible! Leave me alone, all of you!" He was hot with anger; Kaufmann left. Lenz was upset.

On the following day Kaufmann wanted to go. He persuaded Oberlin to accompany him to Switzerland. The wish to become personally acquainted with Lavater,[3] whom he had long known by correspondence, decided him. He accepted; they had to spend one day on preparations. To Lenz this was a burden. In order to rid himself of his immeasurable torment he had clung anxiously to every person and thing around him.

3. J. G. Lavater (1741–1801), the Swiss theologian and moralist, famous in his lifetime for his physiognomical writings. His *Aphorisms on Man* were annotated by William Blake, who greatly admired his writings. Goethe's attitude to him was more critical. (Transl.)

At certain moments it was clear to him that he was merely deceiving himself; he treated himself like a sick child. Some thoughts, some violent emotions he could not ward off without intense anxiety; then again he would suddenly be driven back to them with boundless urgency, he would tremble, his hair almost on end, until the enormous tension left him exhausted. He took refuge in a vision always hovering in front of his eyes, and in Oberlin whose words, whose face were unutterably soothing to him. So he awaited Oberlin's departure with fear.

The prospect of being left alone in the house at present was dreadful to him. The weather had turned mild, he decided to go with Oberlin into the mountains. On the other side, where the valleys became plains, they separated. He returned alone. He rambled over the mountains in various directions. Vast surfaces sloped down to the valleys, little wooded country, nothing but mighty lines and, further away, the wide, misty plain; in the air a powerful wind, not a trace of human life other than an occasional hovel—used by shepherds in summer, but now deserted—nestling against the slope. He grew calm, almost, perhaps, as if lost in a dream: everything seemed to melt, merged in a single line, like a rising and sinking wave between heaven and earth; he imagined he was lying on the shore of a boundless ocean that softly rose and fell. Sometimes he would sit down; then move on, but slowly, dreaming. He did not look for a way.

It was dark when he came to an inhabited cottage on the slope leading down to the Steintal. The door was locked; he went to a window, drawn by a streak of light. A lamp illuminated little more than a single point: its light fell upon the pale face of a girl who, her eyes half-closed, slowly moving her lips, rested behind it. Further away in the dark an old woman sat singing out of a prayerbook, her voice harsh and throaty. After much knocking she opened the door; she was half-deaf. She served Lenz with some food and showed him a place where he could sleep, but never ceased chanting her song. The girl had not stirred. Some time later a man came in; he was tall and lean, traces of gray hair, with a restless, troubled face. He went up to the girl, she started and became restless. He took a dried herb from the wall and laid its leaves on her hand, so

that she grew more quiet and hummed intelligible words in
long-drawn, but piercing tones. The man told her how he had
heard a voice in the mountains and had then seen sheet-
lightning above the valleys; he had been seized bodily too and
had wrestled with it like Jacob. He went down on his knees and
prayed softly but fervently, while the sick woman sang in long-
drawn, softly echoing tones. Then he settled down for the
night.

Lenz dozed dreamily, but later heard the clock ticking in
his sleep. The rushing of the wind made itself heard through
the girl's low chanting and the old woman's voice, sometimes
close, sometimes distant, and now bright, now clouded over,
dreamlike the moon cast its changing light into the room. At
one time the singing became louder, the girl spoke words both
definite and distinct: she said that on the rock opposite there
stood a church. Lenz looked up: she was sitting upright behind
the table, her eyes wide open, and the moon shed its light upon
her features, from which a ghostly glow seemed to radiate; at
the same time the old woman muttered hoarsely, and amidst
this changing and sinking of the light, these sounds and voices,
Lenz at last fell into a deep sleep.

He awoke early. In the half-light of the room all were
asleep, even the girl had found some rest. She was leaning
back, her hands folded under her left cheek; the ghostly glow
had faded from her face, her expression now was one of
indescribable suffering. He stepped up to the window and
opened it, the cold morning air struck his face. The house was
situated at one end of a low, narrow valley which opened
toward the east; red rays shot through the gray morning sky
into the half-light of the valley, deep in white mist, sparkled
against gray stones, and pierced the windows of the huts. The
man awoke. His eyes met a candle-lit picture on the wall and
remained fixed upon it, without a flicker; now he began to
move his lips and prayed softly, then loudly, then more loudly
still. Meanwhile some people entered the hut and, without so
much as a word, fell upon their knees. The girl was suffering
from convulsions, the old woman was rattling out her song and
chatting with the neighbors. The people told Lenz that the
man had come to this district a long time ago, no one knew

where from, he was reputed to be a saint, he could see water underground and exorcise evil spirits, and people went on pilgrimages to see him. At the same time Lenz discovered that he had strayed farther from the Steintal; he left together with a party of woodcutters who were going toward those parts. He was glad of the company; he now felt uneasy in the presence of that powerful man, who sometimes seemed to him to be talking in horrible tones. Also he was afraid of himself when in solitude.

He came home. But the night now past had left a deep impression. The world had been bright, and now he felt in himself a stirring and teeming toward an abyss into which a relentless power was dragging him. Now he was burrowing within himself. He ate little; many nights half-spent in prayer and feverish dreams. A violent surging, and then beaten back exhausted; he lay bathed in the hottest tears and then suddenly acquired a strange strength, rose cold and indifferent; his tears seemed like ice to him then, he could not help laughing. The higher he raised himself by his efforts, the deeper down he was hurled again. Once more everything converged into one stream. Recollections of his old state of mind convulsed him and threw searchlights into the wild chaos of his mind.

In the daytime he usually sat in the room downstairs. Madame Oberlin went in and out of the room; he sketched, painted, read, clutched at every diversion, always hurriedly changing from one to another. But he felt particularly drawn to Madame Oberlin's company, when she was sitting there, the black hymnbook in front of her, next to a plant that had been reared inside the room, the youngest child between her knees; also he gave much attention to the child. Once he was sitting like this when he grew anxious, jumped up and began to walk about. The door ajar—then he heard the maid sing, unintelligibly at first, later he heard these words:

> "In this world I have no joy at all
> But my sweetheart, and he's away."

This struck home, the words and the intonation almost destroyed him. Madame Oberlin looked at him. He took heart, could no longer endure to be silent, he had to speak about it: "Dearest Madame Oberlin, couldn't you tell me what's

become of the lady[4] whose fate lies so heavy on my heart?"
—"But, Herr Lenz, I don't know anything about it."

Then he was silent once more and began to pace the room,
briskly from one end to the other and back again; but soon he
paused to say: "Look here, I'll leave; O God, you're the only
people with whom I could bear to live, and yet—and yet I
must go, to *her*—but I can't, I mustn't." He was greatly
excited and left the house.

Toward evening Lenz returned, the room was in twilight,
he sat down beside Madame Oberlin. "You see," he resumed,
"when she used to walk through the room, singing half to
herself, and every step she took was a kind of music, there
was so much happiness in her, and that overflowed into me,
and I was always at peace when I looked at her or when she
leaned her head against me, and—she was wholly a child; it
seemed as if the world were too wide for her, she was so
retiring, she would look for the narrowest place in the whole
house, and there she'd sit as though all her happiness were
concentrated into one little point, and then I thought so too;
then I could have played like a child. Now I feel so hemmed
in! So restricted! You see, sometimes I feel my arms colliding
with the sky; oh, I'm suffocating! And often at those moments
I think I'm suffering physical pain, there, in the left side, in
my arm with which I used to hold her. And yet I can no longer
picture her, the image runs away from me, and that torments
me; only at times everything becomes clear and bright, and I
feel quite well again." Later he often returned to this subject
when speaking to Madame Oberlin, but always incoherently;
she could not reply at great length, but consoled him a little.

Meanwhile his religious torments continued. The emptier,
the colder, the more dead he felt inwardly, the more he was
urged to kindle some kind of heat within; he remembered the
times when everything seethed within him, when the ardor
of all his emotions made him breathless. And now so dead!

4. In 1772, at Sesenheim near Strasbourg, Lenz made himself
ridiculous by courting Friederike Brion, for no other reason, it was
said, than that Goethe had done so before him. One of Lenz's finest
poems, *Die Liebe auf dem Lande*, deals with this episode; it should
have served to vindicate his sincerity. (Transl.)

He despaired of himself; then he went down on his knees, he wrung his hands, he stirred up everything that was in him—but all was dead, quite dead! Then he implored God to give him a sign, to work a miracle through him; then he tormented himself, fasted, lay on the floor in a dream.

On the third of February he heard that a child had died at Fouday; Friederike was her name. He took this up like a fixed idea. He withdrew to his room and fasted for one day. On the fourth he suddenly entered Madame Oberlin's room; he had smeared his face with ashes and demanded an old sack. She was startled but gave him what he wanted. He wrapped the sack around himself like a penitent and set out for Fouday. The people in the village were already used to him; many a strange tale about him had circulated there. He entered the house where the dead child lay. The people were going about their business indifferently; he was shown to a room, the child was lying on straw placed on a wooden table, dressed in her shift.

Lenz shuddered when he touched her cold limbs and saw the half-open, glassy eyes. The child seemed so forsaken, and he himself so feeble and lonely. He threw himself down upon the dead body. Death frightened him, a violent agony overcame him; these features, this still face would have to decay—he went down on his knees, he prayed with all the anguish of despair that God might work a miracle through him and recall the child to life, weak and unhappy though he was: then he withdrew into himself and concentrated all his willpower upon one point. For a long time he sat there motionless. Then he rose and clasped the child's hands in his and said loudly and earnestly: "Arise and walk!" But soberly the walls echoed his voice, as though to mock him, and the corpse remained cold. Half-mad, he collapsed on the floor; then terror seized him, he rushed out and away into the mountains.

Clouds were passing swiftly across the moon; now all was in darkness, now the nebulous, vanishing landscape was revealed in the moonlight. He ran up and down. In his breast Hell was rehearsing a song of triumph. The wind sounded like the singing of Titans. He felt capable of clenching an enormous fist, thrusting it up into Heaven, seizing God and dragging

Him through His clouds; capable of masticating the world with his teeth and spitting it into the face of the Creator; he swore, he blasphemed. Thus he arrived at the highest point of the mountains, and the uncertain light stretched down toward the white masses of stone, and the heavens were a stupid blue eye, and the moon, quite ludicrous, idiotic, stood in the midst. Lenz had to laugh loudly, and as he laughed atheism took root in him and possessed him utterly, steadily, calmly, relentlessly. He no longer knew what it was that had moved him so much before, he felt cold; he thought he would like to go to bed now, and went his way through the uncanny darkness, cold and unshakable—all was empty and hollow to him, he was compelled to run home, and went to bed.

On the following day he felt intense horror when he remembered his condition on the previous night. Now he stood on the brink of the abyss, where a mad desire urged him to look into its depths again and again and to repeat this torment. Then his fear increased, for what confronted him was nothing less than the sin against the Holy Ghost.

Some days later Oberlin returned from Switzerland much sooner than expected. Lenz was upset by this. But he became more cheerful when Oberlin told him about his friends in Alsace. Oberlin walked about the room, unpacked his things, put them away. He came to talk about Pfeffel,[5] praising the happiness of a country parson's life. Also he proceeded to advise Lenz to comply with his father's wishes, to take up his profession again, to return home. He told him: "Honor thy father and thy mother," and more in this strain. The conversation violently disquieted Lenz; he sighed deeply, tears welled from his eyes, he spoke abruptly: "Yes, I know, but I can't bear it; do you want to drive me away? In you alone is the way to God. But it's all over with me! I've fallen away. I'm damned for eternity, I'm the Wandering Jew." Oberlin told him that this was precisely what Jesus had died for, that he should turn to Him with fervor and would then partake of His mercy.

5. G. C. Pfeffel (1736–1809), the author of poems and fables popular at one time, lived at Colmar. (Transl.)

Lenz raised his head, wrung his hands and said: "Ah! Divine consolation!" Then, suddenly gracious, he asked what had become of the lady. Oberlin replied that he knew nothing whatever about her, but that he would help him in all things; but Lenz must inform him of the place, circumstances, and of her identity. Lenz answered incoherently: "Oh, she's dead! Is she still alive? You angel! She loved me, I loved her, she was worthy of it—you angel! This damnable jealousy, I sacrificed her—she loved another man also—I loved her, she was worthy of it—O dear mother, she also loved me. I'm a murderer!" Oberlin replied that perhaps all these persons were still alive, contentedly perhaps; whatever their condition now, once Lenz had been wholly converted in his heart, God could and would do so much for them in answer to his prayers and tears that the service he would have done them would perhaps outweigh the harm he had already done. This gradually calmed Lenz, who went back to his painting.

In the afternoon he returned to Oberlin. On his left shoulder he had placed a piece of fur, and in his hand he carried a bunch of birch rods, which he had been asked to deliver to Oberlin together with a letter. He gave the rods to Oberlin and asked him to beat him with them. Oberlin took them from him, kissed him several times on the mouth, and said: "These are the only strokes I can give you." He asked him to calm himself and to make his peace with God by himself, as any number of scourgings could not remove a single sin; Jesus had made that His business, and it was to Him that Lenz should turn. Lenz went away.

During supper he was, as usual, somewhat pensive. Yet he spoke of one thing and another, but with anxious haste. At about midnight Oberlin was awakened by a noise. Lenz was running through the courtyard, calling out the name "Friederike" in a hollow, metallic voice, though in confusion and despair; he flung himself into the basin of the fountain, splashed about in it, out again and up to his room, down again to the fountain, and continued in this way several times. At last he grew quiet. The maids, who lived in the nursery immediately below his room, said they often, but particularly during this same night, heard a moaning sound which they

could compare only with the sound of a reed pipe. Perhaps it
was Lenz whining in a hollow, terrible, despairing voice.

Next morning Lenz did not appear at the usual time. At last
Oberlin went up to his room; Lenz was lying in bed, rigid and
motionless. Oberlin had to address him several times before he
received an answer; at last Lenz said: "Yes, Vicar, you see, it's
boredom, boredom! Oh, it's very boring! Really. I no longer
know what to say. I've already drawn all sorts of figures on the
wall." Oberlin told him to direct his thoughts toward God,
whereupon Lenz laughed and said: "Yes, if I were as fortunate
as you are, fortunate enough to find such a pleasant pastime,
yes, in that case I imagine you could fill in the time quite
pleasantly. All out of idleness: for most of us pray out of
boredom, others fall in love out of boredom, some are virtuous,
and some are evil; only I am nothing, nothing, and I don't
even feel like doing away with myself; it really is too boring!

> "O God, in the wave of thy light,
> At thy noontide's glistening height,
> My long-waking eyes have grown sore.
> Shall the healing light come no more?"

Oberlin looked at him with displeasure and prepared to go.
Lenz flitted after him, fixing him with a ghastly look: "You
see, now I have an idea after all, if I could only distinguish
whether I'm dreaming or awake; you see, it's very important,
we must look into it." Then he flitted back into bed.

In the afternoon Oberlin wished to pay a visit in the neigh-
borhood. His wife had already left. He was about to leave
when someone knocked on the door, and Lenz came in, his
body bent forward, his head hanging down; his whole face and
part of his clothing covered with ashes, his left hand supporting
his right arm. He asked Oberlin to pull his arm, since he had
twisted it in the act of throwing himself out of the window;
but since nobody had seen him do it, he did not want anyone
else to know. Oberlin was violently shocked, but said nothing;
he did what Lenz had asked him to do. Immediately after-
ward he wrote to the schoolmaster at Bellefosse, asking him
to come down, and giving him instructions; then he rode
away.

The man arrived. Lenz had often seen him before and had become attached to him. The schoolmaster pretended he had come to discuss certain matters with Oberlin and would then leave. Lenz asked him to stay, and so they remained together. Lenz suggested a walk to Fouday. He visited the grave of the child whom he had once tried to raise from the dead, knelt down several times, kissed the earth on the grave, seemed to be praying, but confusedly plucked up some of the flowers that grew on the grave, to keep as a souvenir, returned to Waldbach, turned back again, and Sebastian with him. Sometimes he walked slowly and complained of a great weakness in his limbs, then again with desperate haste; the landscape frightened him, it was so narrow that he was afraid of colliding with every object he could see. An indescribable feeling of discomfort came upon him, his companion began to be a burden to him; also, perhaps, he guessed his intentions, and now tried to get rid of him. Sebastian seemed to give in to him, but found secret means of informing his brother of the danger, and now Lenz had two keepers instead of one. He continued to drag them along with him; at last he returned to Waldbach, and as they approached the village, turned about quick as lightning and bounded away like a stag in the direction of Fouday. While they were looking for him at Fouday, two shopkeepers approached them and told them that a stranger who confessed that he was a murderer had been arrested in one of the houses and had been bound, but that surely he could not be a murderer. They ran to the house and found it so. A young man, intimidated by Lenz's violent insistence, had bound him. They released him and brought him safely to Waldbach, where they found Oberlin and his wife, who had returned in the mean time. Lenz looked confused. But when he found that his reception was kind and affectionate, his courage revived; his face changed favorably, he thanked his two escorts politely, even tenderly, and the evening passed quietly. Oberlin persistently implored him not to take any more baths, to remain in his bed, and to rest during the night, and, if he could not sleep, to converse with God. He promised, and did so the following night. The maids heard him pray almost all night long.

The following morning he went up to Oberlin's room in a
cheerful mood. When they had discussed various matters, he
said with extreme gentleness: "Dearest vicar, the lady of
whom I was telling you has died, yes died—the angel!"—
"How do you know that?"—"Hieroglyphics, hieroglyphics!"
Then not another word could be got out of him. He sat down
to write some letters and gave them to Oberlin, asking him to
add a few lines to them.

Meanwhile his condition had become increasingly hopeless.
All the peacefulness he had drawn from Oberlin's companion-
ship and the valley's stillness was gone; the world which he
had wished to put to some use had suffered an immense rift;
he felt no hatred, no love, no hope—a terrible emptiness, and
yet a torturing restlessness, an impatient impulse to fill this
void. He possessed nothing. What he did he did unconsciously
and yet under the compulsion of an inner urge. When he was
alone he felt so horribly lonely that he constantly talked, called
out to himself in a loud voice, and then again he was startled
and it seemed as though a stranger's voice had spoken to him.
In conversation he frequently stuttered, an indescribable fear
possessed him, he had lost the conclusion of his sentence; then
he thought he must hold on to the word he had last spoken,
say it again and again, and it was only with greatest exertion
of his will that he suppressed these impulses. The good people
were deeply grieved when sometimes, in his quieter moments,
he sat with them and spoke without difficulty, and then
suddenly began to stammer and an unspeakable fear was
expressed in his features, when convulsively he seized the
person nearest to him by the arm, and only gradually recovered
himself. When he was by himself or reading a book, it was
even worse; all his mental activity was often held up by a
single word. If he thought about a stranger or if he pictured
that person vividly to himself, then it was as if he himself
became that person; he became utterly confused, and at the
same time he felt an unending urge to do violence in his mind
to every thing and person; nature, men, and women, only
Oberlin excepted—all was dream-like, cold. He amused himself
by mentally turning the houses upside down, dressing and
undressing people, by thinking out the most extravagant

pranks. Sometimes he felt an irresistible urge to carry out whatever project he happened to be hatching in his head, and then he made the most horrible faces. Once he was sitting next to Oberlin, the cat was lying opposite him on a chair. Suddenly his eyes became fixed, he kept them riveted upon the animal; then slowly he slipped off his chair, likewise the cat; it seemed to be spellbound by his gaze, grew immensely frightened, arched and bristled its back in terror, Lenz making catlike sounds, his face ghastly, distorted; as though in desperation they hurled themselves at each other, till at last Madame Oberlin rose to separate them. Then again he was deeply ashamed of himself. His nocturnal torments increased terribly. It was only with the greatest difficulty that he could go to sleep at all after first trying to fill the terrible void. Then between sleep and waking he fell into a dreadful state; he collided with some gruesome thing, it was horrible, madness clutched at him; he started up, bathed in sweat, uttered the most piercing shrieks, and only gradually came to himself again. Then he had to begin with the simplest objects in order to come to his senses. Really it was not he who did so, but a powerful instinct of self-preservation; he seemed to be split in two, with one part of him trying to save the other and calling out to itself; gripped by the most violent fear, he would recite poems again and again or tell himself stories until he recovered himself.

Even in the daytime he had these attacks, and then they were still more terrible; previously daylight had saved him from them. Then it seemed to him that he alone existed, that the world was only a figment of his imagination, that there was nothing but he himself, and he the eternally damned, Satan, left to himself and to his painful imaginings. He tore through his past life with blinding speed, and then said: "Consequential, consequential;" if somebody spoke, he said: "Inconsequential, inconsequential;"—it was the cleft of irremediable madness, a madness throughout eternity.

The urge for self-preservation would surprise him, he would fling himself into Oberlin's arms, cling to them as though he wanted to take refuge inside him. Oberlin was the only person who was alive to him and through whom life was still revealed to him. Then gradually Oberlin's voice would recall him to his

senses; he would kneel down before him, his hands resting in
Oberlin's hands, his face covered with cold sweat but resting
on Oberlin's lap, his whole body trembling and heaving.
Oberlin's pity for him was endless, the family were on their
knees, praying for Lenz in his misery, the maids ran away and
took him for one possessed. And when he grew calmer his
sorrow was like a child's; he sobbed, he felt deep, deep compassion for himself; and these were his happiest moments.
Oberlin spoke to him about God. Lenz quietly freed himself
and looked at him with an expression of infinite suffering,
finally saying: "But if I were almighty, you see, if I were that,
I should not tolerate all this suffering, I should save, save; for
all I want is peace, peace so that I can sleep a little." Oberlin
told him this was blasphemy. Lenz shook his head discon-
solately.

His half-hearted attempts at suicide, which occurred
regularly during this period, were not wholly serious. It was
not so much the desire for death—since for him there was
neither peace nor hope in death—as an attempt to recall
himself to consciousness through physical pain, in moments of
terrible fear or of a blank calm that bordered on nonexistence.
Those times at which his mind seemed to be riding on some
weird and eccentric idea were still his best. Then at least he
was almost at peace, and his wild eyes were not as terrifying
as in those moments of fear seeking for salvation, as in his
unending torment of unrest. Often he beat his head against the
wall or in some other way caused himself violent physical pain.

On the morning of the eighth he remained in bed. Oberlin
went to see him; he lay there almost naked and was greatly
excited. Oberlin wished to cover him, but Lenz complained
bitterly, saying that all was so heavy, so very heavy! that he
did not think he could walk at all, that never before had he
felt the immense weight of the air. Oberlin told him not to
be afraid, but Lenz remained in the same position and would
not stir during the greater part of the day, nor would he take
any food.

Toward evening Oberlin was called away to see a sick person
at Bellefosse. The weather was mild and the moon was out.
On his way home he met Lenz, who seemed quite reasonable

and spoke to Oberlin in a calm and friendly manner. Oberlin asked him not to go too far away; he promised. As he was moving off, he suddenly turned about, came quite close to Oberlin and said quickly: "You see, vicar, if only I didn't have to listen to that any more, I'd be cured."—"Listen to what, my dear fellow?"—"Can't you hear it then? Can't you hear the terrible voice that is crying out the whole length of the horizon and that is usually known as silence? Ever since I came to the quiet valley I've heard it incessantly, it won't let me sleep; yes, vicar, if only I could sleep again some day!"— Then, shaking his head, he moved on.

Oberlin returned to Waldbach, intending to send somebody back for Lenz, when he heard him walk up to his room. A moment later something burst in the courtyard with such a mighty noise that Oberlin thought it could not possibly be caused by the fall of a human body. The nursemaid came up to him, deathly pale and trembling all over . . .

With cold resignation he sat in the carriage as they drove west along the valley. He did not care where they were taking him. Several times, when the carriage was endangered by the roads, he remained sitting there, perfectly calm; he did not care at all. In this state of mind he passed over the mountains. Toward evening they reached the Rhine valley. They gradually left the mountains behind; now like a crystal wave the mountains rose against the red sky, a deep blue crystal wave on whose warm flood the red rays of evening played; a shimmering, bluish web covered the plain at the foot of the mountain range. It grew darker as they approached Strasbourg; a high, full moon, all the more distant landmarks in darkness, only the mountain nearest to them still in sharp relief; the earth was like a golden cup over which the gold waves of the moon ran foaming. Lenz stared at it all, not an idea, not an emotion, inside him; only a blunted fear that grew more intense as the landmarks lost themselves more and more in the darkness. They had to turn in for the night. Then once again he made several attempts to lay hands on himself, but he was too well guarded.

On the following morning, in dull, rainy weather, he arrived in Strasbourg. He seemed quite reasonable, and talked to all sorts of people. He did everything just as the others did; but there was a terrible emptiness inside him, he no longer felt any fear, any desire, his existence was a burden to him, a burden he must bear.

So he lived on . . .

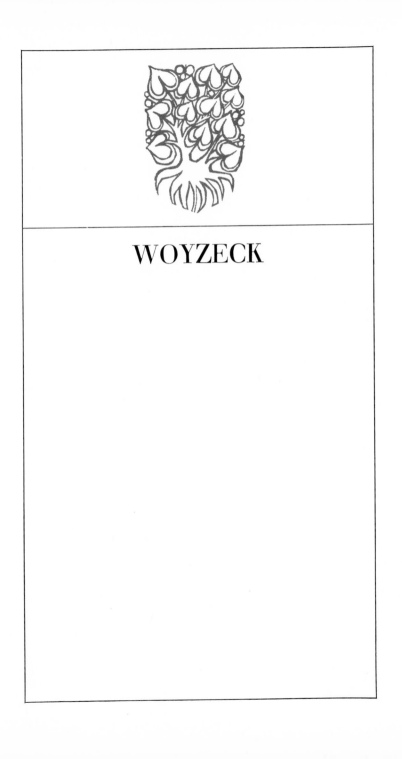

WOYZECK

PERSONS

WOYZECK · MARIE

CAPTAIN · DOCTOR

DRUM MAJOR · CORPORAL

ANDRES · MARGRET

BOOTH OWNER · BARKER

OLD MAN WITH A BARREL ORGAN

JEW · INNKEEPER

FIRST JOURNEYMAN

SECOND JOURNEYMAN

KATE · KARL, an idiot

GRANDMOTHER

FIRST, SECOND, THIRD CHILD

FIRST, SECOND PERSON

POLICE INSPECTOR

AT THE CAPTAIN'S

CAPTAIN *in a chair.* WOYZECK *shaving him*

CAPTAIN: Steady on, Woyzeck, steady on; one thing at a time. You make me quite giddy. What am I going to do with the ten minutes by which you'll be finishing early today? Think of it, Woyzeck: you still have a good thirty years to live, thirty years! That makes three hundred and sixty months; and the days! the hours! the minutes! What do you imagine you're going to do with that enormous amount of time? Everything in its turn, I say, Woyzeck.

WOYZECK: Yes, Captain, sir.

CAPTAIN: I get quite worried about the world, when I think of eternity. To keep occupied, Woyzeck, to keep occupied! Eternal—that means eternal, that means eternal—you understand that; but then again it is not eternal, and that's a moment, yes, a moment—Woyzeck, I shudder at the thought that the world comes full circle in a day! What a waste of time! What's the point of it? Woyzeck, I shall never see another mill wheel turn without falling into melancholia.

WOYZECK: Yes, Captain, sir.

CAPTAIN: Woyzeck, you always look so harassed. A good man doesn't look harassed, a good man with a clear conscience.— Say something, then, Woyzeck! What's the weather been like today?

WOYZECK: Bad, Captain, bad: wind!

CAPTAIN: I can sense it, Woyzeck, there's something quick outside. A wind like that has the same effect on me as a mouse. (*Craftily.*) I think we have something blowing from the south-north. Eh, Woyzeck?

WOYZECK: Yes, Captain, sir.

CAPTAIN: Ha, ha, ha! That's a good one, south-north! Ha, ha, ha. Oh, you're stupid, quite abominably stupid.—(*Mawkishly.*) Woyzeck, you're a good man—but (*With dignity.*) Woyzeck, you have no morals. Morals, that means when a man is moral, you understand, it's a good word. You have a child without the blessing of the Church, as the most reverend Chaplain of our garrison puts it—without the blessing of the Church, the phrase is not mine.

WOYZECK: Captain, almighty God in His goodness won't look at the poor little brat to see whether Amen was said over him before he was made. Our Lord said: suffer little children and forbid them not to come unto me.

CAPTAIN: What's that you are saying? What a strange answer! You're making me quite confused by answering like that. When I say you, I mean you, you—

WOYZECK: Us poor people—you see, Captain: money, money. If a man has no money—just let him try to reproduce his kind in a moral sort of way! We're made of flesh and blood like other people. Our sort will always be unblessed in this world and the next. I think that if we went to Heaven we'd have to help make thunder.

CAPTAIN: Woyzeck, you have no virtue! You are not a virtuous man. Flesh and blood? When I lean out of the window, after rain, and just watch those white stockings go by, as they skip down the street—damn it, Woyzeck, then I feel love rise in me! I too have my flesh and blood. But virtue, Woyzeck, virtue! How should I pass the time in that case? I always say to myself: you're a virtuous man (*Mawkishly.*), a good man, a good man.

WOYZECK: Yes, Captain, virtue, sir—I haven't got the hang of it, up to now. You see: us common folk, our sort don't have any virtue, we just feel the call of nature; but if I was a gentleman and had a hat and a watch and a frock coat and could talk refined, I'd be virtuous all right. It must be a fine thing, virtue, sir. But I'm a poor man.

CAPTAIN: All right, Woyzeck. You're a good man, a good man. But you think too much. That eats you up. You always look so harassed. Our conversation has quite upset me. Be off now, and don't run so fast. Steady on, nice and slowly down the street.

OPEN FIELD, THE TOWN IN THE DISTANCE

WOYZECK *and* ANDRES, *cutting sticks in the scrub.*

ANDRES: (*Whistles.*)

WOYZECK: Yes, Andres, the place is accursed. Do you see that bright streak over the grass where the toadstools keep shooting up? There the head rolls at nightfall. One day someone lifted it up, he thought it was a hedgehog: three days and three nights, and that man lay on the wood shavings. (*Softly.*) Andres, those were the Freemasons. That's it, the Freemasons!

ANDRES: (*Sings.*)

> There sat a couple of hares
> Cropping the green, green grass . . .

WOYZECK: Quiet! Can you hear it, Andres? Can you hear it? Something is abroad!

ANDRES: (*Sings.*)

> Cropping the green, green grass
> Down to the turf.

WOYZECK: It's moving about behind me, beneath me. (*Stamps on the ground.*) Hollow, do you hear? All hollow down there! The Freemasons!

ANDRES: I'm scared.

WOYZECK: It's so uncannily quiet. Makes you want to hold your breath.—Andres!

ANDRES: What?

WOYZECK: Say something. (*Stares into the countryside.*) Andres! How bright it is. Above the town all's aglow. A fire sweeps over the sky and a great noise comes down as of trombones. How close it's coming!—Let's go, quick! Don't look behind you. (*Pulls him into the scrub.*)

ANDRES: (*After a pause.*) Woyzeck, can you still hear it?

WOYZECK: It's quiet, all quiet, as though the world was dead.

ANDRES: Listen! They're drumming inside. We must go.

THE TOWN

MARIE *with her* CHILD *at the window.* MARGRET. *The tattoo marches past, the* DRUM MAJOR *at the head.*

MARIE: (*Rocking the child in her arms.*) Hey, boy. Ta-ra-ra-ra! Do you hear them? Here they come!

MARGRET: What a figure of a man! Like a tree, he is!

MARIE: He stands on his feet like a lion. (DRUM MAJOR *salutes them.*)

MARGRET: Oh, what a come-hither look you gave him, neighbor. That isn't like you.

MARIE: (*Sings.*)

> Soldiers, those are handsome men . . .

MARGRET: Why, your eyes are still bright—

MARIE: What if they are! You take your eyes to the jeweler and have them polished; maybe he'll make them bright enough to be sold for a pair of buttons.

MARGRET: What, you? You saying that to me? You, Mrs. Spinster? I'm a respectable person, but you, everyone knows what you are, you can look right through seven pairs of leather breeches!

MARIE: Slut! (*Breaks a windowpane.*) Come on, my boy. Let them say what they like. That's right, you're only a poor son of a whore and make your mother glad with your illegitimate face. Rockaby! (*Sings.*)

> Girl, what now will you do?
> You have a child but no man!
> Oh, well, why should I care?
> I'll sing the whole night through,
> Hey, ho, my boy, and hurray!
> It's nobody's business but mine.

(*A knock at the window.*) Who's there? Is it you, Franz? Come in.

WOYZECK: Can't. Have to go on parade.

MARIE: Did you cut sticks for the Captain?

WOYZECK: Yes, Marie.

MARIE: What's wrong with you, Franz? You look so distraught—

WOYZECK: (*Mysteriously.*) Marie, something was there again, a lot—isn't it written: And behold, smoke rose up from the land, like unto smoke from a furnace?

MARIE: Pull yourself together, man!

WOYZECK: It followed behind me as far as the outskirts of the town. Something we can't grasp, can't understand, something that drives us out of our minds. What will become of us?

MARIE: Franz!

WOYZECK: I must go.—Tonight at the fair. I've saved up a bit of money again. (*He goes.*)

MARIE: That man! So haunted. Never looked at his child. He'll crack up with all that thinking!—Why do you keep so mum, boy? Are you scared? It's getting so dark, anyone would think he was blind. Usually that lamp shines into this room. I can't bear it; I feel creepy. (*Exit.*)

BOOTHS. LIGHTS. PEOPLE

OLD MAN: (*Sings, and* CHILD *dances to the barrel-organ.*)
> In this world there is no staying,
> Each one of us must die,
> And knows it when he says good-bye.

WOYZECK: Hey, there! Hop along!—Poor man, poor old man. Poor child, poor little child. Cares and merrymaking!

MARIE: Man, if even fools are rational, then we ourselves are fools.—Funny world! Beautiful world! (*Both walk on to the* BARKER'S *place.*)

BARKER: (*In front of his booth with his* WIFE *in trousers and a dressed-up monkey.*) Gentlemen, gentlemen! Look at this creature, as God made it: nothing, nothing at all. Then look at art: walks upright, wears jacket and trousers, carries a sword. The monkey's a soldier; that isn't much, true, the lowest rank of the human race. Come on, give us a bow! That's right—now you're a lord. Blow us a kiss! (*He blows a trumpet.*) The fellow is musical. Gentlemen, here you will see the astronomical horse and our famous little cannery birds. They're popular with all the crowned heads of Europe, telling people everything: how old, how many children, what illnesses. The performance is about to begin. We are just opening the commencement of the commencement.

WOYZECK: Do you want to?

MARIE: All right. It must be a fine show. All those tassels on the man! And the woman has trousers on! (*Both enter the booth.*)

DRUM MAJOR: Halt, there! Do you see her? What a figure of a woman!

CORPORAL: Never seen one like her. Fit to reproduce whole regiments of guardsmen!

DRUM MAJOR: And to breed drum majors!

CORPORAL: How she carries her head! One would think her black hair would drag her down like a lead weight. And those eyes—

DRUM MAJOR: As though you were looking down a wellshaft or a chimney. Let's go. After her!

MARIE'S BEDROOM

MARIE: (*Sitting, the* CHILD *on her lap, a bit of looking glass in her hand.*) The other fellow gave him an order, and he had to go. (*Looks in the mirror.*) How those precious stones glitter! What kind are they? What did he call them?— Sleep, boy. Close your eyes, tight. (*The child hides his eyes behind his hands.*) Tighter still. Stay like that—quite still, or he'll get you. (*Sings.*)

> Girl, shut your shop now.
> Here comes a gypsy boy
> To lead you by your hand
> Off into Gypsyland.

(*Looks in the mirror again.*) It's sure to be gold. How will it look on me when I'm dancing? Our sort have nothing but a little corner in this world and a little bit of mirror, and I have lips as red as those great ladies with their looking-glasses as tall as they are and their handsome gentlemen who kiss their hands. I'm only a poor woman. (*The child sits up.*) Keep still, boy, and shut your eyes. The little angel of sleep—look how he's running along the wall. (*She makes the glass flash.*) Shut your eyes, or he'll peer into them and make you blind. (*Enter* WOYZECK, *stepping behind her. She starts, putting her hands to her ears.*)

WOYZECK: What's the matter with you?

MARIE: Nothing.

WOYZECK: But there's something glittering under your fingers.

MARIE: A little earring. I found it.

WOYZECK: I've never found anything like that—not a pair of them together.

MARIE: Am I a whore?

WOYZECK: All right, Marie.—How the boy sleeps. Lift him up a bit, the chair is hurting his arm. There are bright beads on his forehead, nothing but work under the sun, even in sleep we sweat. Us poor people!—Here's some money, Marie: my pay and a tip from the Captain.

MARIE: May God reward you, Franz.

WOYZECK: I must be off. Tonight, Marie. Good-bye.

MARIE: (*Alone, after a pause.*) I *am* a whore all right. I could stab myself for it.—Oh, what a world! With everyone going to the devil, man and woman alike.

AT THE DOCTOR'S

WOYZECK. THE DOCTOR.

DOCTOR: I'm disappointed in you, Woyzeck—a man as good as his word.

WOYZECK: How, Doctor, I don't know what you mean, sir.

DOCTOR: I saw you, Woyzeck. You pissed in the street, pissed against the wall like a dog.—And yet those three pennies daily and your diet, Woyzeck, that's bad. The world is getting bad, very bad.

WOYZECK: But, Doctor, the call of nature!

DOCTOR: Call of nature, call of nature, my foot! Nature! Haven't I proved that the *musculus constrictor vesicae* is controlled by the will? Nature indeed! Woyzeck, in each and every human being nature is sublimated into freedom. —And you say you're incapable of holding your water? (*Shakes his head, folds his hands behind him, and paces the room.*) Have you eaten your peas, Woyzeck? Nothing but peas, *cruciferae*, remember. There will be a revolution in science, I'm going to blow it sky-high. *Urea* O, 10, hydrochloric ammonium, hyperoxydol—Woyzeck, don't you need to piss again? Just go in there and try.

WOYZECK: Doctor, I can't, sir.

DOCTOR: (*With emotion.*) But you *can* piss against the wall!

I have it in writing, the contract is here.—I saw it myself, with my own two eyes. I'd stuck my nose out of the window, letting the sunbeams drop into it, to observe the phenomenon of sneezing. (*Walks up to him.*) No, Woyzeck, I refuse to be angry: anger is unhealthy, unscientific. I am calm, quite calm. My pulse rate is the normal sixty, and I'm talking with the greatest composure. God forbid that one should get angry about a man, a mere man! If it were a proteus, at least, an amoeba that was dying on one—that would be a very different matter. But, Woyzeck, you shouldn't have pissed against the wall—

WOYZECK: Well, sir, you see, Doctor, sometimes one has a certain character, a certain structure. But nature is different, you see; nature (*He snaps his fingers.*), that's something, how shall I put it, for instance . . .

DOCTOR: Woyzeck, you're philosophizing again.

WOYZECK: (*Confidingly.*) Doctor, have you ever come across dual nature? When the sun is at the zenith and it's as though the world was going up in flames, it has happened that a terrible voice spoke to me.

DOCTOR: Woyzeck, you have an *aberratio.*

WOYZECK: (*Laying a finger on his nose.*) The toadstools, Doctor, that's where it is. Have you ever observed the configuration that toadstools make on the ground by their growth? If only one could make it out!

DOCTOR: Woyzeck, you have the most beautiful *aberratio mentalis partialis*, of the second order, very clearly defined. Woyzeck, you will receive a bonus. Second order: *idées fixes*, in a condition generally sane.—You're still doing everything as before? Still shaving your Captain?

WOYZECK: Yes, sir.

DOCTOR: Eating your peas?

WOYZECK: Regularly as ever, sir. The housekeeping money goes to my wife.

DOCTOR: Doing your fatigues?

WOYZECK: Yes, sir.

DOCTOR: You're an interesting case. Subject Woyzeck, you will get your bonus, just do your duty. Let me feel your pulse. That's right, as I thought.

MARIE'S BEDROOM

MARIE. DRUM MAJOR.

DRUM MAJOR: Marie!

MARIE: (*Looking him in the face, expressively.*) Just take a few steps, will you? Like a bull across his chest, and bearded like a lion. There's no man like him. I am exalted above all women!

DRUM MAJOR: Just wait till Sunday, when I wear my great plumes and my white gloves. That will be something. The Prince always says, "Look at that fellow! That's what I call a man."

MARIE: (*Tauntingly.*) I don't believe a word of it. (*Going up to him.*) Man!

DRUM MAJOR: And you're quite a woman, too. Heaven above, let's found a race of drum majors. Eh? How about it? (*He puts his arms around her.*)

MARIE: (*Suddenly ill-humored.*) Let go of me!

DRUM MAJOR: Wild animal!

MARIE: (*Vehemently.*) Just try to lay hands on me!

DRUM MAJOR: Is the devil peeping out of your eyes?

MARIE: All right, then. It's all the same.

STREET

CAPTAIN. DOCTOR. CAPTAIN *wheezes down the street, stops; wheezes, looks around.*

CAPTAIN: Don't run like that, Doctor. Don't paddle around in the air with your cane like that. You're chasing your own death, doing that. A good man. . . . (*He grabs the Doctor's coat.*) Doctor, allow me to save a human life.

DOCTOR: In a hurry, Captain, in a hurry.

CAPTAIN: Doctor, I'm so melancholic, there's something dreamy about me. I'm always moved to tears when I see my tunic hang on the wall.

DOCTOR: Hm. Blubbery, fat, thick neck: apoplectic constitution. Yes, Captain, you could easily get an *apoplexia cerebri*; but you could also get it only on one side and be paralyzed there, or, if you're lucky, you could be mentally paralyzed and vegetate on like that. Those, roughly, are your prospects for the next four weeks. However, I can assure you that your case is among the more interesting, and if it is God's will that your tongue be partly paralyzed, we shall make the most immortal experiments.

CAPTAIN: Doctor, don't frighten me. People have died of shock before now, of sheer, unadulterated shock. I can already see those persons with lemons in their hands; but they will say, he was a good man—you coffin-nail devil.

DOCTOR: (*Holds out his hat to him.*) What's that, Captain? That's a hollow head, most honorable parade cock.

CAPTAIN: (*Shows him a pin.*) And what's that, doctor? That's a nitwit, most gracious Mr. Coffin-Nail. Ha, ha, ha! But never mind. I'm a good man, but I can, when I want to, Doctor, when I want to . . . (WOYZECK *appears and wants to hurry past them.*) Hey, there, Woyzeck, why do you rush past us like that? Stay a moment, Woyzeck. Why, you're running through the world like an open razor, you cut people! You run as though you had to shave a regiment of new *castratos* and were going to be hanged for the longest hair even before the operation. But, à propos long beards, what was I going to say? Long beards, Woyzeck . . .

DOCTOR: A long beard under the chin, even old Pliny mentions it, should be discouraged among soldiers . . .

CAPTAIN: (*Continues.*) Hah, about long beards! How is it, Woyzeck, haven't you yet found a hair from a beard on your plate? You know what I'm driving at, don't you? A hair of a man, from the beard of a sapper, a corporal, a—drum major? Eh, Woyzeck? But you have a good wife. You don't have that trouble, like other people.

WOYZECK: Yes, sir. What's that you're saying, Captain?

CAPTAIN: What a face the fellow's making! Maybe not in your soup, but if you hurry and go round the corner, perhaps you'll still find one on a pair of lips. A pair of lips, Woyzeck. I too have felt love, Woyzeck. Oh, the fellow's turned as white as chalk!

WOYZECK: Captain, sir, I'm a poor devil—and have nothing else in the world. Captain, if you're having a joke . . .

CAPTAIN: A joke? I? It's your joke, fellow.

DOCTOR: Your pulse, Woyzeck, your pulse! Faint, hard, sporadic, irregular.

WOYZECK: Captain, sir, the earth is as hot as Hell—I'm cold as ice, frozen—Hell is cold, I bet you. Impossible! Whore! Whore! Impossible.

CAPTAIN: Fellow, do you want—do you want a couple of bullets in your head? You're stabbing me with your eyes, and I'm well disposed toward you because you're a good man, Woyzeck, a good man.

DOCTOR: Facial muscles tense, stiff, at times twitching. Bearing excited, tense.

WOYZECK: I'm going. Much is possible. Human beings! Much is possible. It's fine weather we're having, Captain, sir. Look at it, such a fine, solid, gray sky. One could feel tempted to hammer a wedge into it and hang oneself from it, only because of the little dashes between yes and yes again—and no, Captain, yes and no? I'll think about it. (*Leaves with long strides, slow at first, then faster and faster.*)

DOCTOR: (*Rushes after him.*) Phenomenal! Woyzeck, a bonus!

CAPTAIN: It makes me quite giddy to see them—men! How fast? The long knave stretches his legs like the shadow of a spider's legs, and the short one, he's toddling along. The tall one is lightning, and the little one is thunder. Ha, ha! Grotesque! Grotesque!

MARIE'S BEDROOM

MARIE. WOYZECK.

WOYZECK: (*Stares at her and shakes his head.*) Hm, I don't see anything, I don't see anything. Oh, one ought to be able to see it, to put one's hands on it and grasp it.

MARIE: (*Intimidated.*) What's wrong with you, Franz? It's your brain, Franz, you're raving.

WOYZECK: A sin, that thick and that wide—it stinks so much, you could smoke the little angels out of Heaven with it. Your mouth is red, Marie. Is there no blister on it? Eh, Marie, you're beautiful as sin—can deadly sin be so beautiful?

MARIE: Franz, you're delirious.

WOYZECK: The devil! Did he stand here? Like this? Like this?

MARIE: Since the day is long and the world is old, many people can stand in the same place, one after the other.

WOYZECK: I saw him.

MARIE: One can see many things, if one has a pair of eyes in one's head and isn't blind and if the sun is shining.

WOYZECK: Whore! (*Goes for her.*)

MARIE: Just you dare lay hands on me, Franz. I'd sooner have a knife in my belly than your hand on mine. My father didn't dare take hold of me when I was ten years old, if I looked him in the eyes.

WOYZECK: Woman! No, something would have to show on you. Every human being is like an abyss: it makes one dizzy to look down into it. Well, it could be. She walks like innocence personified. Well, innocence, you are branded with a sign. Do I know? Do I know? Who knows? (*Exit.*)

THE GUARDROOM

WOYZECK. ANDRES.

ANDRES: (*Sings.*)

> Our lady has a virtuous maid,
> She sits in the garden all day, all night,
> She sits in her bower's shade . . .

WOYZECK: Andres!

ANDRES: Well?

WOYZECK: Fine weather.

ANDRES: Sunday weather—music outside town. The women-folk went out there a little while ago. The trollops are steaming, they're out for a good time.

WOYZECK: (*Disturbed.*) A dance, Andres; they're dancing.

ANDRES: At the White Horse and the Three Stars.

WOYZECK: Dance, dance.

ANDRES: If you like. (*Sings.*)

> She sits in her bower's shade.
> Until the little bell strikes twelve,
> And she watches out for soldiers.

WOYZECK: Andres, I'm feeling so restless.

ANDRES: Old fool!

WOYZECK: I must go out there. Everything's turning in front of my eyes. Dance, dance! How hot her hands will be! A curse on it, Andres!

ANDRES: What are you after?

WOYZECK: I've got to go out, to see.

ANDRES: You jack-in-the-box! Because of the whore?

WOYZECK: I must get out, it's so hot in here.

INN

The windows open. Dancing. Benches in front of the inn.
JOURNEYMEN.

FIRST JOURNEYMAN: (*Sings.*)
>   I'm wearing a shirt, it isn't mine;
>   My soul reeks of brandy, my soul reeks of wine . . .

SECOND JOURNEYMAN: Brother, out of sheer friendship shall I punch a hole for you in nature? Let's go. I want to punch a hole in nature. I'm a man, too, as you know. I want to beat the life out of every flea on his body.

FIRST JOURNEYMAN: My soul reeks, my soul reeks of brandy and wine. Even money rots in the end. Forget-me-not, how beautiful is this world! Brother, I shall have to fill a rain barrel with my blubbering, I'm so sad! I wish our noses were a couple of bottles and we could pour them down each other's gullet.

OTHERS: (*In unison.*)
>   One day a huntsman rode
>   All merry through the green, green wood.
>   Halloo, halloo, how happy is the huntsman's way
>   Here on the green, green heath.
>   To hunt is all my joy.

(WOYZECK *goes to the window.* MARIE *and the* DRUM MAJOR *dance past without noticing him.*)

WOYZECK: Him! Her! The devil!

MARIE: (*Dancing past.*) On and on, on and on.

WOYZECK: (*Stifling.*) On and on, on and on! (*Jumps to his feet and sinks back on to the bench.*) On and on, on and on!

(*Claps his hands together.*) Yes, keep turning, tumbling! Why doesn't God blow out the sun, so that everyone and everything can tumble together higgledy-piggledy, man and woman, man and beast? Do it in broad daylight, do it on people's hands like gnats! Woman! The woman is hot, hot! On and on; on and on! (*Starts up.*) That fellow, how he fingers her, all over her body! He's got her—as I had her at the start. (*He sinks back, dazed.*)

FIRST JOURNEYMAN: (*Preaching from the table top.*) Albeit, when the wanderer who standeth leaning against the current of time or else answereth to himself the divine wisdom and speaketh unto himself, "Wherefore is man? Wherefore is man?" But verily I say unto you: by what should the farmer, the plasterer, the cobbler, the doctor have lived if God had not created man? By what should the tailor have lived if God had not implanted in man the sense of shame, by what the soldier, if God had not provided man with the need to kill his kind? Therefore be not doubting—indeed, it is lovely and good, but all that is earthly is evil, even money rots in the end. In conclusion, my beloved brethren, let us piss over the Cross so that somewhere a Jew will die. (*Amid general howling* WOYZECK *wakes up and rushes away.*)

OPEN FIELD

WOYZECK: On and on, on and on! Swish, swosh, that's how the fiddles go and the pipes. On and on, on and on! Hush, music. What's speaking down there? (*Puts his ear to the ground.*) Eh, what's that, what are you saying? Louder, louder! Stab, stab the she-wolf to death? Stab, stab the— she-wolf to death! Should I? Must I? Do I hear it down there too? Does the wind say it too? Do I hear it all the time, do the voices keep on and on: stab her, stab her to death, to death!

A ROOM AT THE BARRACKS

Night. ANDRES *and* WOYZECK *in bed.*

WOYZECK: (*Softly.*) Andres!
ANDRES: (*Mutters in his sleep.*)

WOYZECK: (*Shakes Andres.*) Hey there, Andres! Andres!

ANDRES: All right, all right. What is it?

WOYZECK: I can't sleep. When I close my eyes everything keeps turning, and I hear those fiddles, on and on, on and on. And then a voice speaks from the wall. Can't you hear anything?

ANDRES: Yes—let them dance. Someone is sleepy, and then God preserve us, amen.

WOYZECK: It keeps saying: stab, stab, and flashes between my eyes like a knife.

ANDRES: Go to sleep, blockhead. (*He goes back to sleep.*)

WOYZECK: On and on; on and on.

THE DOCTOR'S COURTYARD

STUDENTS *and* WOYZECK *downstairs, the* DOCTOR *at the attic window.*

DOCTOR: Gentlemen, I am up on the roof like David when he saw Bathsheba; but I see nothing but the *culs de Paris* of the girls' boarding school hung up to dry in the garden. Gentlemen, our topic is that important question, the relationship between subject and object. If we take only one of those things in which the organic self-affirmation of the divine manifests itself from so high a vantage-point and examine its relations to space, to the earth, to the planetary —Gentlemen, if I throw this cat out of the window: how will that phenomenon react to the center of gravity in accordance with its own instinct?—Hey, Woyzeck. (*Roars.*) Woyzeck!

WOYZECK: (*Catches the cat.*) Doctor, it's biting me!

DOCTOR: Fellow, you're handling that beast so tenderly, anyone would think it was your grandmother. (DOCTOR *comes down.*)

WOYZECK: Doctor, I have the jitters.

DOCTOR: (*Delighted.*) Good, Woyzeck, very good. (*He rubs his hands. Then he takes the cat.*) What is this I see, gentlemen, the new species of hare's louse, a fine species . . . (*He takes out his magnifying glass; the cat runs away.*) Gentlemen, the animal has no scientific instinct . . . But I'll show you something else instead. Look at this man: for a quarter of a year he's been eating nothing but peas; observe the effects; just feel his irregular pulse. And his eyes!

WOYZECK: Doctor, I'm going to have a blackout. (*He sits down.*)

DOCTOR: Courage, Woyzeck. Only a few more days, and it will be over. Feel it, gentlemen, feel it! (*They finger his forehead, pulse, and chest.*) By the way, Woyzeck, just show these gentlemen how you wriggle your ears. I've long wanted to show you that; two muscles are active with him. —Come on, Woyzeck, look lively!

WOYZECK: Oh, Doctor!

DOCTOR: Animal, do you want me to move your ears for you? Do you want to behave like the cat? There you are, gentlemen. This is some sort of transition to the donkey, frequently the consequence of female rearing and of the mother tongue. How many hairs did your mother tear out of your head as a keepsake, out of tenderness? Your hair has got quite thin in the last few days. Yes, gentlemen, those peas!

BARRACKS SQUARE

WOYZECK: Didn't you hear anything?

ANDRES: He's there, and he's brought a friend.

WOYZECK: He said something.

ANDRES: How do you know? Why should I tell you? All right, then: he laughed, and then he said: a gorgeous woman! Those thighs of hers, and all so hot!

WOYZECK: (*Quite Coldly.*) Oh, so that's what he said. What was it I dreamed of last night? Wasn't it of a knife? What silly dreams one has.

ANDRES: Where are you off to, mate?

WOYZECK: To fetch wine for my officer. But, Andres, there's no denying it, she was a jewel of a girl.

ANDRES: Who was?

WOYZECK: Nothing. See you later. (*Exit.*)

INN

Drum Major. Woyzeck. People.

Drum Major: I'm a real man! (*Beats his chest.*) A real man, I say. Anyone want me to prove it? If he isn't a drunken Lord God Almighty he'd better keep away from me. I'll beat his nose into his arsehole! I'll—(*To* Woyzeck.) Drink up there, fellow. I wish the world was made of gin: gin is a man's drink. (Woyzeck *whistles.*) Fellow, do you want me to pull out your tongue and wrap it round your body? (*They wrestle;* Woyzeck *loses.*) Shall I leave you as much wind as an old woman's fart, shall I? (Woyzeck *sits down on a bench, exhausted and trembling.*) I'll make the fellow whistle a dark-blue tune. (*Sings.*)

> Brandy and gin, they are my life.
> Brandy and gin give courage!

A Girl: He's had his lot.

Another: He's bleeding.

Woyzeck: One thing after another.

JUNK SHOP

Woyzeck. The Jew.

Woyzeck: The little pistol is too dear.

Jew: Well, take it or leave it. Who cares?

Woyzeck: How much is the knife?

Jew: It's as straight as could be. Do you want to cut your throat with it? Well, so what? I'll let you have it as cheaply as I would another man. You're to have your death at a fair price, though not for nothing. What's it about? Let him have an economical death.

Woyzeck: That can cut more than bread.

Jew: Twenty cents.

Woyzeck: There you are. (*Exit.*)

Jew: There you are! As though it was nothing! And yet it's money.—You swine!

MARIE'S BEDROOM

IDIOT *lies on the ground, telling himself fairy tales on his fingers.*

IDIOT: He has the golden crown, His Majesty the King . . .
Tomorrow I'll go and get Her Majesty the Queen's child . . .
Pork Sausage says: come along, Liver Sausage . . .

MARIE: (*Turning the pages of her Bible.*) "Neither was guile
found in his mouth . . ." Lord God, Lord God, do not look
at me! (*Turns the pages.*) "And the scribes and Pharisees
brought unto him a woman taken in adultery; and when
they had set her in the midst . . . And Jesus said unto her,
Neither do I condemn thee; go, and sin no more." (*Claps
her hands together.*) Lord God, Lord God, I cannot . . .
Lord God, only give me so much that I can pray! (THE
CHILD *nestles up against her.*) That child stabs my heart.
(*To the* IDIOT.) Karl, that foulness preens itself in the sun!
(IDIOT *takes the* CHILD *and falls silent.*) Franz didn't come,
not yesterday, not today. It's getting hot here. (*She opens
the window and reads again.*) "And stood at his feet behind
him weeping, and began to wash his feet with tears, and
did wipe them with the hairs of her head, and kissed his
feet, and anointed them with the ointment . . ." (*Strikes
herself on the breast.*) All dead! My Savior, my Savior!
I want to anoint your feet.

BARRACKS

ANDRES. WOYZECK *is rummaging in his kit.*

WOYZECK: That little vest, there, Andres, isn't army issue.
It'll come in useful to you, Andres.

ANDRES: (*Utterly listless, says to all this.*) All right.

WOYZECK: The crucifix is for my sister, and that little ring.

ANDRES: All right.

WOYZECK: I've also got a picture of a saint, two bleeding
hearts and fine gold—it lay in my mother's Bible, and on
it is written:

> Lord, as thy flesh was red and sore
> So let my heart be evermore.

My mother feels nothing now except when the sun shines on her hands—it will do no harm . . .

ANDRES: All right.

WOYZECK: (*Produces a sheet of paper.*) Friedrich Johann Franz Woyzeck, private soldier, rifleman in the Second Regiment, Second Battalion, Fourth Company, born on the Day of the Annunciation, July Twentieth. Today my age is thirty years, seven months, and twelve days.

ANDRES: Franz, you must report sick. Poor fellow, you'll have to drink brandy with a powder in it; that's a cure for fever.

WOYZECK: Well, Andres, when the carpenter sweeps up those wood shavings, no one knows who will lay his head on them.

STREET

MARIE *with* GIRL *in front of the porch*, GRANDMOTHER; *later*, WOYZECK.

GIRL: (*Singing.*)
> Bright shines the sun at Candlemas,
> The tall corn stands in flower.
> They marched along the meadowside,
> They marched in twos and twos.
> The pipers marched at the head,
> The fiddlers marched behind,
> The socks on their feet were red . . .

FIRST CHILD: That's a nasty song.

SECOND CHILD: You're never satisfied.

FIRST CHILD: Marie, you sing for us.

MARIE: I can't.

FIRST CHILD: Why can't you?

MARIE: Because.

SECOND CHILD: But *why* because?

THIRD CHILD: Grandmother, *you* tell us a story.

GRANDMOTHER: Come here, then, you little shrimps.—Once upon a time there was a poor child, and it had no father and no mother; all were dead, and no one left in the world. All dead, and it went out and searched by day and by night. And because there was no one left on this earth, it wanted to go to Heaven, and the moon gave it such a kind look; and when at last it got to the moon, the moon was a bit of rotten wood. And it went to the sun, and when it came to the sun, the sun was a wilted sunflower. And when it came to the stars, they were little golden midges, and those were impaled, as the shrike impales them on sloe thorns. And when it wanted to go back to earth, the earth was an upside-down pot. And it was quite alone. And so it sat down and wept, and there it still sits and is quite alone.

WOYZECK: (*Appears.*) Marie!

MARIE: (*Starts.*) What is it?

WOYZECK: Marie, let's go. It's time.

MARIE: Where to?

WOYZECK: Who knows?

WOODLAND PONDSIDE

MARIE *and* WOYZECK.

MARIE: So the town is out yonder. It's dark.

WOYZECK: You're to stay a while. Come on, sit down.

MARIE: But I must go.

WOYZECK: You won't get sores on your feet walking.

MARIE: I can't make you out at all.

WOYZECK: Have you any idea how long it's been now, Marie?

MARIE: Two years at Whitsun.

WOYZECK: And do you know how much longer it will be?

MARIE: I must go and cook supper.

WOYZECK: Do you feel the chill, Marie? And yet you're so warm. How hot your lips are! Hot, hot with a whore's breath. And yet I'd give all Heaven to be able to kiss them just one more time . . . Do you feel the chill? When one's cold one doesn't feel the chill anymore. The morning dew won't chill you.

MARIE: What are you getting at, Karl?

WOYZECK: Nothing. (*Silence.*)

MARIE: How red the moon is rising.

WOYZECK: Like a bloody blade.

MARIE: What's on your mind, Franz, you're so pale. (*He raises the knife.*) No, Franz, don't! In Heaven's name, help, help!

INN

WOYZECK: Dance, the lot of you, on and on! Sweat and stink! He'll get you anyway in the end, every one of you! (*Sings.*)

> Oh, daughter, my dear daughter,
> What made you do it, when
> You gave yourself to the country coachmen
> And those cart and carriage men?

(*He dances.*) There, Kate, sit down. I'm feeling hot, hot. (*He takes off his tunic.*) That's how it is, the Devil takes one woman and lets the other go scot-free. Kate, you're hot. Why? Kate, you too will be cold one day. Be sensible. Can't you sing?

KATE: (*Sings.*)

> That southern country I can't bear,
> Long dresses never I will wear,
> For full-length gowns and pointed shoes
> No decent servant girl will choose.

WOYZECK: That's right, no shoes, one can go to Hell without shoes.

KATE: (*Sings.*)

> Shame on you, love, for that low tone.
> No, keep your money and sleep alone.

WOYZECK: Yes. Truly, I don't want any blood on me.

KATE: But what's that on your hand?

WOYZECK: On me? On me?

KATE: Red! It's blood. (PEOPLE *surround them.*)

WOYZECK: Blood? Blood?

INNKEEPER: Ooh—blood!

WOYZECK: I think I must have cut myself, there on my right hand.

INNKEEPER: Then how did it get on to your elbow?

WOYZECK: I wiped it off.

INNKEEPER: What, wiped it off the right hand on to the right elbow? You must be a bleeding contortionist!

IDIOT: And then the giant said: "I smell the blood of an Englishman." Pooh, it's begun to stink.

WOYZECK: To Hell with you! What do you want of me?

What business is it of yours? Out of my way, or the first . . .
To Hell with you! Do you think I've done somebody in?
Am I a murderer? What are you gaping for? Stare at
yourselves for a change. Out of my way there! (*He runs
away.*)

AT THE PONDSIDE

WOYZECK *alone.*

WOYZECK: The knife? Where's the knife? I left it over there.
It will give me away. Nearer, still nearer! What sort of
place is this? What's this I hear? Something is stirring. All
quiet!—Just there—Marie? Ha, Marie! Quiet, all quiet!
Why are you so pale, Marie? Why do you wear a red
necklace around your throat? From whom did you earn it
with your sins? You were black with them, black. Did I
blanch you? Why does your hair hang so wild? Didn't
you plait it today?—The knife, the knife! Have I got it?
That's it. (*He runs to the water.*) That's it, throw it down
there. (*He throws the knife in.*) It goes down in the dark
water like a stone.—No, the place is too shallow, when they
go bathing. (*He wades into the pond and throws it far away.*)
That's better—but in summer, when they dive for mussels?
Oh, it'll be so rusty, no one will recognize it . . . If only
I'd broken it up!—Am I still bloody? I must wash. Here's
a stain, and another there . . . (*People arrive.*)
FIRST PERSON: Stop!
SECOND PERSON: Do you hear it? Quiet! Over there!
FIRST PERSON: Ooh! Over there. What a sound!
SECOND PERSON: It's the water, it's calling out: no one has
drowned here for a long time. Let's go. It isn't good to hear
that sound.
FIRST PERSON: Ooh! There it comes again—like a man
dying!
SECOND PERSON: It's uncanny. So misty, a hazy gray every-
where—and the hum of beetles like cracked bells. Let's go!
FIRST PERSON: No, it's too clear, too loud. Up there! Follow
me!

CHRONOLOGY OF GEORG BÜCHNER'S
LIFE AND WORK

17 October 1813. Born at Goddelau near Darmstadt, as the eldest child of Dr. Ernst Büchner, a physician, and Caroline Büchner (née Reuss). Of Georg's brothers and sisters, Ludwig Büchner became eminent as a doctor and as the author of *Force and Matter*, *Man and his Place in Nature*, and *Mind in Animals*, important studies in evolution and animal psychology; Wilhelm Büchner as a research chemist and Reichstag deputy; Alexander as a professor of literature in France; Louise as a writer in the feminist cause. Georg's paternal grandfather, too, was a medical man, his favorite uncle on his mother's side, Eduard Reuss, a Lutheran theologian.

1824–1831. Attended school, the *Gymnasium* in Darmstadt.

1831–1833. Studied natural sciences at the University of Strasbourg, where he became secretly engaged to Minna Jaegle, a pastor's daughter.

October 1833. Moved to the University of Giessen, where he took up practical medicine at his father's request, but suffered an illness, diagnosed as incipient meningitis, and had to return home after five weeks. Another serious illness followed in the spring of 1834.

1834. Back at Giessen after convalescence, meeting with Pastor Friedrich Ludwig Weidig, leader of the Liberal movement in Hesse. Büchner joined the Society for the Rights of Man and collaborated with Weidig in the writing of *Der Hessische Landbote*, a pamphlet calling on the peasants to revolt. In April, brief visit to Strasbourg, where Büchner's engagement to Minna Jaegle was made public.

In July, Büchner attended the Badenburg meeting of members of the revolutionary society, a branch of which he had set up in Darmstadt earlier in the year. In August the stock of the *Landbote* was seized by the government, one of Büchner's associates arrested, and Büchner himself interrogated. Continued his studies at home.

1835. Denunciation of the anonymous authors of the *Landbote.* In April, arrest of Pastor Weidig (who committed suicide in prison, where he was tortured, soon after Büchner's death). Büchner wrote *Dantons Tod,* in order to raise money for his secret escape to Strasbourg. Translated Victor Hugo's *Lucrèce* and *Marie Tudor.* An expurgated version of *Dantons Tod* and the two translated plays were published with the help of Karl Gutzkow, leader of the Young Germany movement.

1836. Büchner managed to get to Strasbourg in March, before he was denounced. A warrant for his arrest was issued in June. In Strasbourg he worked on his thesis on the nervous system of the barbel, written in French; also on *Lenz* and on *Leonce und Lena.* The comedy was intended for a competition, but Büchner submitted it too late. Presented his thesis to the *Société d'Histoire Naturelle* of Strasbourg and was made a member of the society. Granted his doctorate by the University of Zürich, which appointed him a lecturer in comparative anatomy of fishes and amphibia. At work on *Woyzeck.* Trial lecture in Zürich on the cranial nerves. Moved to Zürich and took up his appointment in October.

19 February 1837. Died of typhus in Zürich.

1850. First collection of Büchner's works, edited by his brother Ludwig.

1879. Second collection of his works, edited by Karl Emil Franzos.

1902. First performance of *Dantons Tod.*

1911. First performance of *Leonce und Lena.*

1913. First performance of *Woyzeck* (called *Wozzeck* until this misreading of the name was corrected).

1921. Alban Berg's opera *Wozzeck*, based on Büchner's dramatic fragment.

Another play, *Pietro Aretino*, which Büchner is said to have written, has never come to light. One possibility is that his fiancée destroyed the manuscript.

TEXTUAL AND BIBLIOGRAPHICAL NOTE

These translations are based on the text established by Fritz Bergemann for the Insel edition of Büchner: *Werke und Briefe* (7th Edition, Wiesbaden, 1958). The more recent critical edition by Werner R. Lehmann (Vol. 1, Hamburg, 1967) has been consulted, but its reordering of the scenes that make up *Woyzeck* for a proposed new acting version struck me as dramatically weaker than Bergemann's version, which has been adopted on the stage in recent decades. A brief account of the reordering and principal textual variants appears in my notes on *Woyzeck*.

SOME CRITICAL WORKS ON BÜCHNER

In English

A. H. J. Knight: *Georg Büchner*. Oxford, 1951.

Margarest Jacobs: Introduction and notes to *Dantons Tod* and *Woyzeck*. Manchester, 1954.

Michael Hamburger: *Georg Büchner*. In *Reason and Energy*, London and New York, 1957, London, 1971; and *Contraries*, New York, 1970.

Herbert Lindenberger: *Georg Büchner*. Carbondale, Illinois, 1964.

J. P. Stern: *Re-Interpretations*. London, 1964. (Various sections on Büchner.)

In German

Karl Viëtor: *Georg Büchner: Politik. Dichtung. Wissenschaft.* Berne, 1949.

Horst Oppel: *Die tragische Dichtung Georg Büchners*. Stuttgart, 1951.

Walter Höllerer: *Zwischen Klassik und Moderne: Lachen und Weinen in der Dichtung einer Übergangszeit.* Stuttgart, 1958.

Wolfgang Martens: *Ideologie und Verzweiflung: religiöse Motive in Büchners Revolutionsdrama.* Euphorion, Vol. 54, 1960.

Hans Mayer: *Georg Büchner und seine Zeit.* Berlin, 1960.

Georg Büchner: Woyzeck. In the series *Dichtung und Wirklichkeit.* Frankfurt, 1963.

Gerhart Baumann: *Georg Büchner: die dramatische Ausdruckswelt.* Göttingen, 1961.

A NOTE ON *LEONCE AND LENA*

On 3 February 1836, the publishing house of Cotta offered a prize for a comedy written in German, to be submitted by the end of August. Büchner sent in *Leonce and Lena*, but the manuscript, which is not extant, arrived too late and was returned to him unread.

The Italian epigraph, with its pun on "fame" and "hunger," appears to be Büchner's own invention. Its relevance to the play is not obvious, since hunger is touched upon only in Act Three, Scene Two, where the peasants are lined up for the royal wedding and smell roast meat for the first time in their lives. Yet it points to the spirit of realism and social criticism that Büchner insinuated into his superficially romantic comedy, just as the comedies of Carlo Gozzi were realistic in spirit despite their fairy-tale components, as compared to the idealistic tragedies of his contemporary Vittorio Alfieri. Gozzi's comedies may have been among Büchner's models, which also included comedies by Clemens Brentano, Ludwig Tieck, and Alfred de Musset, as well as Shakespeare, to whom the epigraph to the first act refers.

Büchner's extant letters tell us virtually nothing about the works written after *Dantons Tod*, but he mentions what he calls his *Ferkeldramen*—literally, "piglet plays"—probably meaning *Leonce and Lena* and perhaps his lost play about Pietro Aretino, which is likely to have been "indecent" according to the standards of his time. Büchner's spirit of farcical realism, blended throughout *Leonce and Lena* with Jacquesian melancholy, is also suggested by his choice of names for the two kingdoms, childish designations for physical realities unmentionable and "piggish" by the same standards. But it is *Woyzeck* that makes most of the natural needs of the "poor, bare, forked animal." In *Leonce and Lena* Büchner contented himself with making gentle fun of repressive and falsifying decencies. The political satire observes the same restraint. Jokes about the smallness of the two kingdoms take them out of the fairy tale into actuality; they are the little autonomous despotisms into which Germany was divided before 1871.

Büchner's obsession with puppets or automatons and the illusoriness of personal identity is apparent in all his plays, though in *Dantons Tod* and *Woyzeck* it is metaphor, rather than action, that conveys it. Valerio's taking off of successive masks and his fear of peeling and skinning himself until there is nothing left of him anticipates the famous onion metaphor in Ibsen's *Peer Gynt*. Philosophically—and in *Leonce and Lena* Büchner also repeatedly guys the terminology of German idealistic philosophy—the question about personal identity links up with that about free will and determinism. If the identity of individuals is largely a delusion, so is the assertion of their wills. That is one humbling and disturbing implication of the comedy, but one that should be taken as ironically as the rest of the play, since Büchner's hidden spirit of realism turns the play itself into an ironically self-mocking artifice.

As for the utopian or prelapsarian paganism of the conclusion, Büchner may well have given half-serious consideration to its possibilities as an escape from suffering and an alternative to nineteenth-century claptrap about virtue, much as he gave amused consideration to the moral reformism of Saint-Simon in his letter of 27 May 1833. Büchner's Danton and his friends provide a precedent in their readiness to live and let live. Yet Büchner knew better than anyone that no religion, however "comfortable," eliminates the suffering to which his Danton and Camille succumb; and in a later letter (1 January 1836) he dissociated himself from the liberal reformism of the "literary party of Gutzkow and Heine"— which was drawn to Saint-Simonism and to visions of moral emancipation very much like Valerio's in the play—and added: "Also, I am far from sharing their views on marriage and on Christianity."

A NOTE ON *LENZ*

Jacob Michael Reinhold Lenz, the subject of Büchner's story, was a poet and dramatist of the *Sturm und Drang* period. Born in 1751 in the Baltic province of Livonia, the son of a Lutheran clergyman, he studied theology at Königsberg. After two years of rather lukewarm study he gave it up to become private tutor to two young Barons von Kleist, traveling with them to Strasbourg, where he met Goethe. When Goethe left for a journey with one of the Kleist brothers, Lenz was introduced to Friederike Brion, whom Goethe celebrated in some of his best-known love poems, and fell in love with her. Lenz became a figure of fun as "Goethe's ape."

Five years later, in March 1776, Lenz arrived at Weimar, where Goethe had now settled. Goethe did his best to be kind to him, but Lenz behaved so eccentrically that he was asked to leave the dukedom in December. He then visited Goethe's brother-in-law at Emmendingen, moved on to Colmar, staying with G. C. Pfeffel, and then to Switzerland. There, from November 1777 to January 1778, he was the guest of Christoph Kaufmann, a doctor, and suffered his first mental breakdown. Kaufmann sent him to the vicarage of Johann Friedrich Oberlin in the Steintal and later visited Lenz, together with his fiancée, Lisette Ziegler. This is the period of Büchner's story. Although Lenz's mental condition gradually improved after his removal to Strasbourg, he was taken back to Lithuania in 1779, fell into obscurity, and died near Moscow in 1792.

Büchner was interested in Lenz as the author of the plays *Der Hofmeister* (1774, revived in this century in the adaptation by Brecht) and *Die Soldaten* (1776), which served as points of departure for his *Woyzeck*. A collection of Lenz's works, edited by Ludwig Tieck, appeared in 1828, when

Büchner was a schoolboy. In 1831 Daniel Ehrenfried Stöber, the father of two of Büchner's Strasbourg friends, published a biography of Lenz in French. In the same year August Stöber, Büchner's friend, published an essay on Lenz's visit to the Steintal, based on Oberlin's diary. Büchner drew on these publications, but mainly on Oberlin's diary, for the documentary material incorporated into his story.

Though *Lenz* was left unfinished when Büchner died, it seems unlikely that he would have substantially changed the story for publication, or added much to it, with the possible exception of a gap in the narrative after "The nursemaid came up to him, deathly pale and trembling all over." Oberlin's diary gives the reason: Lenz had just made another attempt at suicide by throwing himself out of the window. At this point Oberlin decided that Lenz could not remain in his house. He sent for two men to act as warders until Lenz could be removed to Strasbourg; but before their arrival Lenz tried to stab himself with a pair of scissors. In the course of the night he proved too strong for the two men; a third was called in, but Lenz told them that even three of them would never get the better of him. Oberlin managed to calm him by kindness and by granting Lenz's request to pray for his soul. Later that day Lenz declared himself willing to be taken to Strasbourg and left, as Büchner relates, escorted by the same three men.

A NOTE ON *WOYZECK*

The extant manuscripts of *Woyzeck* consist of unnumbered scenes, or successive drafts of such scenes, and neither their intended sequence nor their definitive text can be established. An exact reproduction and description of the manuscript material is to be found in Georg Büchner: *Sämtliche Werke und Briefe, Historisch-kritische Ausgabe mit Kommentar*, Vol. 1, Hamburg, n.d. (1967). In that volume the editor, Werner R. Lehmann, provides a "reading and stage version" that differs essentially from that adopted by Bergemann and by this translator. The order of scenes proposed by Lehmann is as follows:

1 OPEN FIELD (*The town in the distance.*)
2 THE TOWN
3 BOOTHS. LIGHTS. PEOPLE
4 (MARIE'S) BEDROOM (MARIE *sitting* . . .)
5 AT THE CAPTAIN'S
6 (MARIE'S) BEDROOM (MARIE, DRUM MAJOR)
7 IN THE STREET (MARIE, WOYZECK) Corresponds to MARIE'S BEDROOM (*Stares at her, and shakes his head.*), with textual variants.
8 AT THE DOCTOR'S
9 STREET (CAPTAIN, DOCTOR), with textual variants.
10 THE GUARDROOM
11 INN
12 OPEN FIELD (WOYZECK, *alone.*)
13 NIGHT Corresponds to A ROOM AT THE BARRACKS, with textual variants.
14 INN (DRUM MAJOR, WOYZECK, PEOPLE)
15 JUNK SHOP

16 (MARIE'S) BEDROOM (MARIE, IDIOT)
17 BARRACKS (ANDRES. WOYZECK *rummaging in his kit.*)
18 THE DOCTOR'S COURTYARD
19 MARIE Corresponds to STREET. (MARIE *with* GIRL, *in front of the porch.*)
20 EVENING (*The town in the distance.*) Corresponds to WOODLAND PONDSIDE.
21 PEOPLE COME Corresponds to AT THE PONDSIDE, without Woyzeck's monologue.
22 THE INN (WOYZECK, KATE)
23 EVENING (*The town in the distance.*) Corresponds to Woyzeck's monologue up to *He runs to the water.* With textual variants.
24 WOYZECK AT A PONDSIDE. Corresponds to continuation of Woyzeck's monologue. With textual variants.
25 STREET (CHILDREN), as follows:
FIRST CHILD: Let's go, Mary.
SECOND CHILD: What's up?
FIRST CHILD: Didn't you know? Everyone's gone there already. Someone's lying out there.
SECOND CHILD: Where?
FIRST CHILD: To the left, over the butts in the copse, near the red cross.
SECOND CHILD: Come on, then, quick, so we'll see something before they carry it indoors.
26 BAILIFF. DOCTOR. JUDGE, as follows:
BAILIFF: A good murder, a genuine murder, a fine murder, as fine as you could hope to see, we haven't had one like it for a long time.
27 IDIOT. CHILD. WOYZECK, as follows:
KARL: (*Sits the child on his knees.*) He's fallen into the water, he's fallen into the water, eh, he's fallen into the water.
WOYZECK: Lad, Christian.
KARL: (*Stares him in the face.*) He's fallen into the water.
WOYZECK: Christian, my lad, you'll get a hobbyhorse, gee-up. (*The child resists. To Karl:*) There, go and buy the lad a hobbyhorse.

KARL: (*Stares him in the face.*)
WOYZECK: Hop, hop, horsie.
KARL: (*Exultant.*) Hop, hop, horsie, horsie. (*Runs off with the child.*)

Judging by the various drafts, the extreme brevity of the extant text, and by Büchner's habitual faithfulness to historical facts, it does seem probable that he intended to conclude his play with Woyzeck's arrest and trial. It was accounts of the trial, and of the unsuccessful appeals against the death sentence on the grounds of Woyzeck's insanity, that aroused Büchner's concern with this subject. But what is far more important than Büchner's intentions is to make the material he left as coherent and dramatically effective as possible. The suggestion in Bergemann's version that Woyzeck drowns in the pond rounds off the fragment, whereas Lehmann's version leaves us in suspense.

Nor is there much point in speculations as to whether the existing scenes would have been elaborated in a final version. Just as the prose of *Lenz* owes its power to extraordinary ellisions of normal syntax, which enact Lenz's peculiar way of seeing and feeling, the only *Woyzeck* we know is an abbreviated and condensed play that more than makes up in heightened intensity, vividness, and invocativeness for what it lacks in length.